T0074908

Life in Death

The Focus Animation Series aims to provide unique, accessible content that may not otherwise be published. We allow researchers, academics, and professionals the ability to quickly publish high impact, current literature in the field of animation for a global audience. This series is a fine complement to the existing, robust animation titles available through CRC Press/Focal Press.

Series Editor:

Giannalberto Bendazzi, currently an independent scholar, is a former Visiting Professor of History of Animation at the Nanyang Technological University in Singapore and a former professor at the Università degli Studi di Milano. We welcome any submissions to help grow the wonderful content we are striving to provide to the animation community: giannalbertobendazzi@gmail.com.

Giannalberto Bendazzi; Twice the First: Quirino Cristiani and the Animated Feature Film

Maria Roberta Novielli; Floating Worlds: A Short History of Japanese Animation

Cinzia Bottini; Redesigning Animation United Productions of America

Rolf Giesen; Puppetry, Puppet Animation and the Digital Age

Pamela Taylor Turner: Infinite Animation: The Life and Work of Adam Beckett

Marco Bellano; Václav Trojan: Music Composition in Czech Animated Films

Life in Death
My Animated Films 1976–2020

Dennis Tupicoff

CRC Press
Taylor & Francis Group
Boca Raton London New York

CRC Press is an imprint of the
Taylor & Francis Group, an **informa** business

First Edition published 2022
by CRC Press
6000 Broken Sound Parkway NW, Suite 300, Boca Raton, FL 33487-2742

and by CRC Press
4 Park Square, Milton Park, Abingdon, Oxon, OX14 4RN

CRC Press is an imprint of Taylor & Francis Group, LLC

ISBN: 978-1-032-04220-6 (hbk)
ISBN: 978-1-032-05887-0 (pbk)
ISBN: 978-1-003-19966-3 (ebk)

DOI: 10.1201/9781003199663

Typeset in Minion
by codeMantra

Access the videos: https://www.youtube.com/channel/UCmDIUY9FaU0wo_at1_4W4GA

for Giannalberto Bendazzi (1946–2021):
writer and animation historian, archivist,
teacher, mentor, and friend to so many of us.

Contents

Acknowledgements

After 45 years of making films, and living a life along the way, there are really too many acknowledgements to make, and too many people. In trying to do so, I can only allude to the minds, hearts, and hands that have made all the works, and engaged in all the conversations, that have given me so much pleasure and inspiration. Just a few have found their way into this book and its references. But I can thank directly the many people and organizations who helped make these ten animated films (see their credits in Appendix 1) particularly Fiona Cochrane, my co-producer for many years. And many thanks to my family and friends, especially Lou Hubbard and our daughters Zelda and Anna, for their affection, advice, and patience over the decades.

A different form of this book was written as part of the requirements for a PhD at Deakin University. Thanks to my supervisors Dr Dirk DeBruyn and Dr Lienors Torre for their advice. I'm very appreciative of the careful reading and comments by readers at various stages, including Alan Wilson, Anne Richards, Judith Hall, Lou Hubbard, and Max Bannah. The shortcomings are, of course, my own.

Educated in the law, Giannalbert Bendazzi became a historian and archivist of animation. Educated in history, and briefly an archivist, I became an animation film maker. As a student of comedy Giannalberto would have appreciated the irony of these career paths – and the fact that he did not live to see the publication of this book which he encouraged, and which bears the title he suggested: *Life in Death.*

Author

As writer/director/animator/producer, **Dennis Tupicoff** (1951) has made many films, both animated and live action, and has won many awards, including Grand Prix at Ottawa, Oberhausen, Huesca, Istanbul, Madrid, and New Orleans. His career retrospectives have been screened in Krakow, Berkeley, Poznan, Kecskemet, Seoul, Gothenberg, Melbourne, and Brisbane. His animation work is discussed in histories such as *Animation: A World History* (Bendazzi) and *Animation: The Global History* (Furniss), and in more specialized studies like *Animated Documentary* (Honess Roe), *Animated Realism* (Kriger), and *Australian Animation: An International History* (D&L Torre). He was also featured in Chris Robinson's book as one of the *Unsung Heroes of Animation*. In his standard text *Introduction to Documentary*, Bill Nichols says of the animated *His Mother's Voice*: "It is an extraordinarily powerful piece of filmmaking".

Dennis Tupicoff was Lecturer in Post-graduate Animation at the VCA School of Film and Television (1992–1994). He has lectured, mentored, and taken writing workshops at many universities around the world, and has spoken at many international conferences. He has been invited to residencies at Abbaye Fontevraud (France) and as a Fellow at the MacDowell Colony (USA).

His journal publications include:

"How to write a screenplay with a chainsaw"—*Journal of Screenwriting* 9.3 (2018)

"Radio with pictures (thousands of them): *His Mother's Voice*"—*Cartoons* 1:1 (2005)

Academic:

Bachelor of Arts, University of Queensland 1970
Grad. Dip. Teaching, Kedron Park Teachers College 1973
Grad. Dip. Applied Film & Television (Animation), Swinburne University 1977
Doctor of Philosophy, Deakin University 2021

Preface

A S A YOUNG MAN IN 1974, AFTER HEARING A FUNNY SONG
about death, I decided to learn how to turn it into an animated film. In 2020 I made another animated film, this time
describing a strange vision of life and death from even earlier in
my life: 1968. The years between were spent making many short
films as writer/director, both live action and animation, as well as
commissioned work and teaching.

But my own animated films were always about death. Why? What
made each film—whether it was a cartoon, a documentary about
my own life or someone else's, or a complicated hybrid of several
cinematic forms and stories—address the same dark subject? And
why were the films otherwise so different? Creators are often reluc-
tant to talk about (or worse, explain) what they do; surely the work
should speak for itself. But perhaps another more varied approach,
still using words rather than animated pictures and sound, might
be illuminating for readers—and for me. Finally, I set out to find the
answers to these and related questions by investigating my creative
process, influences, and insights for each film.

From its earliest days, the "life" created in animation has always
been central to its meaning. This book addresses matters of life
and death that arise in animation, particularly in the ten short
films I have written and directed. Ranging from one minute to 25
minutes, the films use various animation and film techniques and
tell stories in different ways. They already tell many more than ten

individual stories; much of their energy comes from sudden leaps in cutting and narrative.

The book is written from the inside, as a practitioner who has spent much of his working life in animation as writer, director, designer, animator, and producer. Starting with the original idea and its development, the discussion of each film has a different primary focus. Drawing on the cultural, critical, and historical background, and with practical experience grappling with these issues as an artist and a human being, I present views of death in some of its many forms, from comic to tragic, as part of animation and therefore as part of life.

Introduction:
Animation: A Matter
of Life and Death

But at my back I always hear
Time's wingèd chariot hurrying near;
And yonder all before us lie
Deserts of vast eternity.

ANDREW MARVELL: "TO HIS COY MISTRESS"
(C1653)[1]

"Why are all your films about death?"

This is the question I'm asked most often about the ten animated films I've made since 1976. The subject of death is often
noted in critical writing on my work: "Dennis Tupicoff doesn't
like death…. He's afraid of it and, based on his animation films,
obsesses on it. While most people call animation, 'the illusion of
life', Tupicoff's films could easily be called 'the reality of death'".[2]
This book addresses that question by discussing their creation,
and how various matters of life and death are reflected both in
that process and in the films themselves, as part of a working life.

Whatever the consolations of belief, as living humans we con-
sciously face the inevitability of death. Towards the end of his

extensive discussion of animation and the special ontological status so often claimed for it as being "the illusion of life", Alan Cholodenko acknowledges that "life is never without death at the same time, even that in a sense we have not one but two deaths—the one which precedes us, the one which awaits us—and a third as well—the one which lives with us".[3] I will discuss the relationship of life and death in my films as it relates to human experience, storytelling, theory and narrative in film, and animation in particular. All ten films were conceived, written, designed, produced, directed, and usually animated by me. Although this is not an autobiography, my own life and implicitly my own consciousness of approaching death are often relevant to the discussion.

Here the films are organized into three broad groups and in roughly chronological order:

- *Cartoons* in the traditional sense of fictional drawn animation

- *Documentaries* rendered in animated (usually non-photographic) form

- *Hybrids* of fiction and documentary, and often also of animation and live action

It might be said that animation—in the form of optical toys and devices and particularly Émile Reynaud's "Théâtre Optique"—preceded the cinema itself. The director Alexandre Alexeieff goes further: "It is legitimate to consider cinema as a particular kind of animation, a sort of cheap, industrial substitute; which was destined to replace the creative work of an artist, such as Émile Reynaud, with photography of human models 'in movement'".[4] Certainly all three types of animated films discussed here appeared quite early and have often developed independently of live action cinema. But animation's varied and vital history is inconceivable without the industrial and creative influence of a live action cinema that transcends mere "photography of human models 'in movement'".

However "cheap" and "industrial" it may be for Alexeieff, any form of live action is also strangely compelling evidence of the

Past and of past lives, as described so differently by many writers over more than a century: Gorky's silent grey shadows of former life (1896),[5] Bazin's sense of cinematic death and immortality (1945),[6] and Mulvey's description of the uncanny in cinema, with "questions that still seem imponderable: the nature of time, the fragility of human life, and the boundary between life and death" (2006).[7] The same questions are embodied in fiction by Serafino Gubbio's human yet mechanical camera-cranking arm in Pirandello's 1915 novel *Si Gira!* (*Shoot!*).[8] Live action was—and is—a different "illusion of life": a recording of life past, but seen in the present. The essayist Yvette Biro honours film as "a curious museum":[9]

> Celluloid records so completely that the insignificant, incidental, and superfluous details also appear on the screen, begging for life…. Experiencing the various aspects of nature in such abundance has a near magical effect: we become aware of the singularity of things and realize that the felt occurrence is never to return again…. (Y)et we have managed to capture it, for however short a moment, to touch it, hold it as it is delayed for a while on its way to its demise.[10]

Whatever the magical "life" so often claimed for it, animation has none of this abundance. Except for welcome mistakes, animation records nothing that has not been placed before the camera or planned and executed as computer graphics, nothing that is not essentially conscious and intentional. Movement and an illusory "life" are achieved but life itself—and death—are elsewhere. Even in "virtual reality", the parameters of its "reality" are fixed and very different from the vast, interconnected yet so often accidental reality of life itself.

In her essay "Inscribing Ethical Space: Ten Propositions on Death, Representation and Documentary", Vivian Sobchack opens up the subject of cinematic death in its various forms.[11] She is primarily concerned with the representation of death in the documentary, and how it differs from the fiction film.

She mentions "animation" only in its old-fashioned usage as a synonym for "movement", not the multivalent but particular cinematic form I'm addressing here. However, Sobchack's analysis of representation also provides a way of looking at animation in terms of life and death, while recognizing the illusions and reality of the cinema. And it begins with a rabbit.

In her discussion of Jean Renoir's *La Règle du Jeu (The Rules of the Game,* 1939), "the film that generated this essay", she mentions the famous hunting scene in which a rabbit is shot.[12] The actual death of this rabbit is followed by the murder of the fictional human "André Jurieu". Sobchack is careful to distinguish the "human character" from the unnamed rabbit:

> (I)t is a real rabbit that we see die in the service of the narrative and *for* the fiction. The human character who dies, however, does so only *in* the fiction…. The rabbit's death violently, abruptly punctuates fictional space with documentary space. Non-fictional or documentary space is thus of a different order than fictional space that confines itself to the screen.[13]

The actor survives; the rabbit does not. As Steve Reinke says of this same sequence, "our poor rabbit dies at least two deaths": the pro-filmic (real) death and the filmic one onscreen.[14] Equally, the actor died only once in the cinematic fiction of *La Règle du Jeu.* No animated character will ever be born in the Paris of 1905, as the "André" actor Roland Toutain was, and die in Argenteuil (Val-d'Oise) in 1977.[15] To that extent we must respect animation's "illusion of life" as truly *illusory* and celebrate its concomitant, the "illusion of death". Despite the emotional power of an animated film like *Watership Down* (Rosen, 1978), no animated character will, like that poor rabbit in *La Règle du Jeu,* lose its life for a fictional narrative.

In Sobchack's sense of fictional and non-fictional space, we might speak of "animation space" in which there is no death, not even the later death of the on-screen actor. (Here we must set aside the question of the human voice in animation, to which we shall return.) This does not mean that, well-directed and with an appropriate narrative and strong characters, the death of an animated character can be without powerful feelings of empathy and even grief. Unlike Sobchack, Reinke extends the discussion to include animation, with the famously affecting death of Bambi's mother in *Bambi* (Hand, 1942). Her (unseen) death at the hands of the (unseen) hunters' rifles is indicated only by a thud on the soundtrack and her absence as Bambi searches for her:

> The film is, of course, notorious for the possibly traumatic effect the death of Bambi's mother has on child viewers. In some ways, hunting and animal death in *The Rules of the Game* is inverted in *Bambi*. The off-screen deaths of cartoon characters can pack an incredible wallop as they raise the spectre of symbolic (and actual) maternal death, while the on-screen death of an actual rabbit is likely to cause a much slighter psychic disturbance, even as it directly raises a complex of moral issues.[16]

Despite its talking animals, *Bambi* is, like most of the Disney features, relatively realistic in its design and fictive world view. In other films, of course, animated "life" can allow complete freedom from death and so much else. Cartoon characters can be spliced and diced, burnt to a blackened crisp, blown up with explosives, inflated till they burst, or flattened by a rock or an Acme anvil. But in the next scene, they can be healthy and whole again, unmarked and ready for more mayhem. Even in wartime training films, as Norman Klein points out, "animation is instructional madness made coherent— controlled anarchy...a strangely intimate, non-threatening way to visualize fear (as in animated movies about the risk of crash landing for passengers while they fly on airplanes). It is a carnival about dying, and coming back to life".[17] Many cartoons are tents at exactly that carnival and could not entertain in the same way if they had to inhabit the "merely" fictional or non-fictional spaces of live action.

My animated films are at another carnival, where the characters stay dead—unless there is a post-mortem slow-motion replay, as in the gunfighter Slim's fatal talent quest performance in *Dance of Death*.

My characters are often real people in animated form: a famous Spanish bullfighter, a Brisbane teenager who has been shot and killed, or myself as a child who shoots birds.

Even my cartoon characters are rarely anthropomorphic. When they mix fantasy and reality in animated form, my films' use of fiction and non-fiction has more in common with a live action film such as *A Matter of Life and Death* (Powell and Pressburger, 1946).

In *AMOLAD* the British poet/pilot Peter jumps from his doomed bomber without a parachute. In his last minutes in the burning cockpit he falls in love with June, the American radio operator on the ground, the last voice he hears. (As a poet he even has time to quote Marvell's lines that begin this Introduction.) After many narrative turns and deliberate ambiguities, culminating in a highly political but other-worldly trial and a simultaneous brain operation on Earth—both with life itself at stake—Peter is allowed to stay alive and enjoy the promise of a long life with June. But this is no "carnival about dying"; Peter's "coming back to life" is clearly exceptional and temporary, justified in mortal terms by successful brain surgery. An inventive mix of Shakespeare and brain injury, mythology and visual effects, fantasy and reality in the shadow of World War II—everything *but* animation, in fact— the story of *AMOLAD* is an old one: the triumph, however temporary, of love over death. Adapting Klein's terms, it is "a strangely intimate, non-threatening way to visualize" death.

Whether fact or fiction, my films claim no victory, however temporary, of love over death. But like *AMOLAD* they roam around many aspects of both life and death: history and memoir, media and popular culture, metaphysical speculations and human situations that are comic and romantic, dramatic and tragic. In this ecumenical spirit various themes, topics, and references will be engaged for each of these ten animated films.

The discussion of each film begins with the origins of the film idea itself. Each film was initiated by me and was triggered by events in my life: a question from my young daughter, a radio interview heard by chance, the memory of a strange visionary experience, a newspaper story, or the announcement of a competition for possible funding. Though it will not be discussed here in any detail, the lack of any Australian funding for short films has in recent years put a severe limit on what can be made, if not on the ideas themselves.

As part of the creation of each film I also discuss how it was written and made, the sometimes difficult decisions that are necessary in the film-making process, and influences on individual films and on my work, in general. Some influences were obvious at the time: the deep and abiding symbolism of the skeleton, for instance. But other themes and observations have—like the connections between the films themselves—become clear only in retrospect.

Whatever the germ of the idea, and however it was developed and eventually produced, each of these films *is* concerned with death. But its presence as a subject takes many forms: television entertainment as a modern dance of death, the developing awareness of death in the mind of a child, the inevitability of death in the ceremony of the Spanish bullfight, the threat of death as wielded by an armed robber, anxiety about personal extinction, speculation about the experience of the moment of death itself, a cartoon afterlife, suicide by chainsaw, and more. Death is as varied and interesting as the life to which it is so often opposed, but which is really its companion.

These films are also about other things. After all, Marvell's "To His Coy Mistress" is not limited by those four lines of approaching death and surrounding nothingness, as quoted above, nor by its later talk of worms and graves. The poem is also a carefully structured argument of seduction in three parts, one that has been made in many a bar, party, or doorway: "*if* only we had more time... *but* let's face it: time is short... *so* come on...". It is laced with wit and flattery, sexual references, and all the poetic gravity and urgency of its expression: *carpe diem* (seize the day). We don't know the response of the woman concerned, or if she ever existed. But we do know that the poem has come down to us from the 17th century, intact and powerful, and that it will outlive us.

For each of the ten films I discuss at least one different topic that is not directly related to death: the *idée fixe* in comedy, the human voice as song, as testament and as filmic element, aspects of the craft of animation, the subjective point of view in cinema, the persistence of memory and the archive, the camera lucida and photography, different narrative structures, and so on. Detailed discussion of so many elements is not exhaustive; many of them overlap and are common to various films. My intention is to illuminate some of the connections between these elements and indeed all the films as a body of work.

At the same time death is—like life—always "hurrying near" as both a light source and as shadows cast by the objects before us. This is as true of live action as it is of animation. But unlike the cinematic ghosts of live action, animation has a life that really is illusory. These moving objects have never lived, so they can never die. They have no history or afterlife outside the cinema. Locked in the film frame, without any remembered past or imagined future, their "lives" depend on the many arts and crafts of animated cinema, and on the very real and mortal lives of all the people devoted to it—frame by frame, year by year—from life to death.

Enter: Bugs Bunny.

NOTES

1 In: Bloom, Harold (ed.) *The Best Poems of the English Language*. New York: Harper Collins, 2004. 172–173.
2 Robinson, Chris. *Unsung Heroes of Animation*. Eastley, UK: John Libbey, 2005. 225.
3 Cholodenko, Alan (ed). *The Illusion of Life: Essays on Animation*. Sydney: Power Publications, 1991. 28.
4 quoted in: Bendazzi, Giannalberto. *Cartoons: One Hundred Years of Cinema Animation*. London: John Libbey, 1994. xx.

5 Quoted in: Adair, Gilbert (ed.) *Movies*. London: Penguin, 1999. 10–13.

6 Bazin, Andre. *What Is Cinema?* Vol.1. Berkeley and Los Angeles: University of California Press, 1967.

7 Mulvey, Laura. *Death 24x a Second*. London: Reaktion Books, 2006. 53.

8 Pirandello, Luigi. *Shoot! (The Notebooks of Serafino Gubbio)*. Sawtry, Cambs: Dedalus, 1990.

9 Biro, Yvette. *Profane Mythology: The Savage Mind of the Cinema*. Bloomington: Indiana University Press, 1982. 54.

10 ibid. 54–55.

11 Sobchack, Vivian. in: *Carnal Thoughts: Embodiment and Moving Image Culture*. Berkeley: University of California Press, 2004. 226–257.

12 ibid. 245.

13 ibid. 245–247 (italics in original).

14 Reinke, Steve. "The World is a Cartoon: Stray Notes on Animation" in: Gehman, Chris and Steve Reinke (eds). *The Sharpest Point: Animation at the End of Cinema*. Toronto: YVZ Books, 2005. 18.

15 https://en.wikipedia.org/wiki/Roland_Toutain retrieved 1-7-20.

16 Reinke, Steve. in: Gehman, Chris and Steve Reinke (eds) op. cit. 17–18.

17 Klein, Norman. "Animation as Baroque" in: ibid. 28.

CHAPTER 1

Cartoons of Life and Death

"What's up Doc?"

—BUGS BUNNY (1940)[1]

Like photography and like film itself, animation was made possible by new technology. But it also inherited the whole history of human artistic expression. Despite—or because of—its various pre-cinema forebears in the dramatic, visual, and plastic arts, animation took time to find its various forms and keeps discovering new ones. But, even with its leaning towards caricature and humour, the dark side of the cartoon sensibility is never far away.

In a *Dream of The Rarebit Fiend* cartoon strip from 1905—thus preceding his animated films—Winsor McCay (as "Silas") starts with a seven-panel sequence showing a burial from the point of view of the corpse in the grave, complete with mordant comments from the officiating clergyman: "Death in this case was a blessing not only to his wife but to the whole community. He was absolutely no good".[2] With its clear visual point of view, dialogue, and action timing it is, like many of the "Rarebit" strips, virtually a

DOI: 10.1201/9781003199663-1

storyboard for an animated film never made. In the seventh panel, black clods of earth start to close the oval-framed view of daylight from the bottom of the grave. Only in the eighth and final panel does the "deceased" wake up from his nightmare, in bed with his wife: "I ate a cheese pie last night. Oh, oh, what a dream!" Later, in *The Sinking of the Lusitania* (1918), McCay was to use animation to document the killing of 1,200 people at sea during World War I. And by 1929 Walt Disney was working in the graveyard with *The Skeleton Dance*, a celebration of animated synchronous sound and a film about death that was, ironically, the very first of his *Silly Symphonies*.

Please Don't Bury Me (1976), the first of three cartoon films discussed here, was triggered by the lyrics of a John Prine song (see Chapter 2). "John" wakes up at the start of the film and then dies in his pyjamas. His body goes through various fantasy adventures concocted by me as a novice and self-taught director/animator: armless herself, Venus de Milo uses John's cartoon arms to fire a machine gun; he saws off the feet of his own corpse in the back of a moving hearse; he is eaten by the Hollywood angels at a cartoon banquet in cinematic Heaven.

Unconcerned, John just walks away from the frenzied feast and goes back to sleep in the Void; he might well wake up, alive, in the morning.

The other two cartoons offer little such hope. In *Dance of Death* (1983), a skeleton presides over a television universe of entertainment with only one End in mind.

In *The Heat, the Humidity* (1999), inexorable fate is demonstrated in the rapid shrinkage and final dissolution of a determined but hapless cartoon bank robber who is only too vulnerable to the tropical weather.

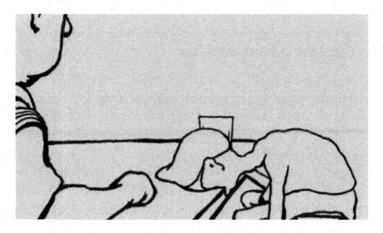

These three films are all fiction—often absurd and without documentary reality—yet they also comment on real human life, culture, and language. They are all about death, and they all have humorous intent.

In Preston Sturges' brilliant farce *Sullivan's Travels* (1941), the eponymous hero has his great moment of realization watching a Disney cartoon. The famous Hollywood director Sullivan finds himself in prison, alone and unknown. As a black choir sings, he files into church with the other criminals and sees *Playful Pluto* (Gillett, 1932). All around him the other prisoners laugh uproariously at the antics of Pluto as he tries to escape a piece of flypaper. Puzzled at first, Sullivan finally joins them in laughter, and it changes his life. This same animation sequence has been widely recognized as a landmark in animation history.[3] The animator Norm "Fergy" Ferguson, a self-taught former camera operator who discovered his gift for drawn animation almost by accident, brings a new level of self-consciousness to drawn comic performance:

> From the time he accidentally sits on a sheet of the stick flypaper, Pluto's problems seem to become ever worse as he tries to extricate himself. Through it all, his reaction to his predicament and his thoughts of what to try next are shared with the audience. It was the first time a character seemed to be thinking on the screen, and though it lasted only 65 seconds, it opened the way for animation of real characters with real problems.[4]

Sullivan himself has the last line in *Sullivan's Travels*, followed by a montage of laughing faces from the Pluto scene and elsewhere: "There's a lot to be said for making people laugh. Did you know that's all some people have? It isn't much, but it's better than nothing in this cockeyed caravan. Boy!"

Ferguson's skill gives the convicts a hilarious and revelatory view of something outside human experience. Pluto's "real" discomfort is the animator's gift: mere drawings that show frustration without cause or consequences, anguish without pain, sheer joy from a cartoon dog's comic encounter with a piece of flypaper. But there are other stories to tell, other territory for "this cockeyed caravan" of life and death. And the animated cartoon can go there too.

NOTES

1 Avery, Tex. *A Wild Hare*. Warner Bros, 1940.
2 Canemaker, John. *Winsor McCay: His Life and Art*. New York: Abbeville Publishers, 1987. 70.
3 Klein, Norman. *Seven Minutes: The Life and Death of the American Animated Cartoon*. London, New York: Verso, 1993. 51.
4 Thomas, Frank and Ollie Johnston. *Disney Animation: The Illusion of Life*. New York: Abbeville Press, 1981. 100.

CHAPTER 2

Please Don't Bury Me (1976)

Woke up this morning
Put on my slippers
Walked in the kitchen
And died.

"PLEASE DON'T BURY ME"—JOHN PRINE[1]

In fact, I woke up this (Saturday) morning in the spring of 1974, in Christchurch, New Zealand. I walked into the city centre and paid $5.95 for *Sweet Revenge*, a vinyl album that changed the course of my life.

A year before, my brother Ross had died after a motor bike accident. Other friends had already died on the roads; I was riding bikes myself and training to be a teacher. A year before that, in London, I had read *Let Us Now Praise Famous Men*.[2] On assignment for *Fortune* magazine, James Agee and Walker Evans had brought their skills in writing and photography to Alabama in the summer of 1936. The article was not published, but 5 years later

DOI: 10.1201/9781003199663-2

they produced this strange book that records, in Agee's words and Evans' pictures, the lives of three white tenant farmer families: their poverty and hopes, squalor and beauty, meanness and grace.

A year before that, in 1971, I was a graduate assistant/researcher at the State Archives in Brisbane, right next to Boggo Road jail. While working there I discovered that my grandfather Nicholas Tupicoff, a young Russian immigrant, had been charged with murder, and acquitted, in 1914. In the small brown paper parcel with the pink ribbon, along with the depositions of witnesses and other records of the case, was a list of his few possessions when he was arrested. While awaiting trial, at the same age as me when I read the file, he had been held in Boggo Road. Only later, after being wounded and gassed in World War I, would he become a poor farmer on one of the hopelessly small and uneconomic "soldier settler" blocks where my father was born, where the family struggled and failed. But the six Tupicoff children were not trapped in poverty like the Alabama tenant farmers; they were all educated and found trades or white-collar jobs. Still, I was the first of my family to go to university. At the end of my first year there, in 1968, I drove a tractor for 5 weeks in the wheat fields of western Queensland. At night I was reading Patrick White's *The Tree of Man*; the elderly couple who owned "Paloma" could have been the novel's Stan and Amy Parker (see Chapter 13).[3]

And here I was in New Zealand, in 1974, after a week's manual work in a door factory, with few possessions or prospects after a short and unhappy teaching career. The stylus hit the grooves of John Prine's *Sweet Revenge*; it was certainly someone else's record player.

> And oh, what a feeling!
> When my soul
> Went through the ceiling
> And on up into heaven I did ride.
> When I got there, they did say
> "John, it happened this-a-way

You slipped upon the floor
And hit your head.
And all the angels say
Just before you passed away
These were the very last words
That you said:

Only here in the chorus does John Prine spell out the darker message to those he has left behind.

Please don't bury me
Down in that cold, cold ground
No, I'd rather have 'em cut me up
And pass me all around.
Throw my brain in a hurricane
And the blind can have my eyes
And the deaf can take both of my ears
If they don't mind the size.

Though it may hint at cannibalism, Prine's comic country song does not have the savage satire or rhetorical power of Jonathan Swift's *A Modest Proposal*.

...a young healthy child well nursed, is, at a year old, a most delicious nourishing and wholesome food, whether stewed, roasted, baked, or boiled; and I make no doubt that it will equally serve in a fricassee, or a ragout.... A child will make two dishes at an entertainment for friends, and when the family dines alone, the fore or hind quarter will make a reasonable dish, and seasoned with a little pepper or salt, will be very good boiled on the fourth day, especially in winter.[4]

Prine was not addressing the social and economic problems that Swift saw in the Dublin of 1729, nor those of Alabama in 1936, nor even those of Nashville in 1973. But the song has echoes of

Stephen Foster's racist minstrel song "Massa's in the Cold Cold ground" (1852), where black slaves mourn the death of their white master.[5] Foster's song was recorded at a funereal pace in 1936 by the all-white Chuck Wagon Gang from Texas.

CHORUS:

> Down in the cornfield
> Hear that mournful sound
> all the darkies are weeping
> Massa's in the cold cold ground.[6]

Though modern and jaunty, the Prine song was in a style that the Alabama tenant farmers of 1936 would have recognized as "country". (And there was a heavenly afterlife too!) But to me in 1974, an unbeliever, it was a funny song about death and its uncomfortable realities, a song that Elvis Presley himself loved before he took his own heavenly ride in 1977.[7] I had not seen—or had no memory of—*Devil May Hare* (McKimson, 1954) the Bugs Bunny cartoon in which the marauding Tasmanian Devil says to Bugs: "What for you bury me in the cold cold ground?" But when I heard "Please Don't Bury Me" I saw it as a cartoon film—and decided to make it.

Around that time I had drawn a simple strip cartoon about creativity and the invention of the Wheel by an ant.

This expression of ironic pessimism did not prevent my strange and immediate decision to animate *Please Don't Bury Me*, nor my spending 2 years to see it through. I knew nothing of how to do animation, and almost nothing about how to make a film. My only experience was filming friends with a borrowed 8 mm camera and, more dangerously, shooting from a motor bike while steering through the viewfinder.

Returning to Australia, I found there was no film school in Queensland. But there was a new Performing Arts course in Toowoomba, a regional city near Brisbane, that had units in film-making. The course was headed by Robert Gist, an American actor and director who had appeared in Hitchcock's *Strangers on a Train* (1951), and had directed the movie of Mailer's *An American Dream* (1966) and a lot of television.[8] He also referred to his friend Marlon Brando as "Marlon" and had once been married to the actor Agnes Moorehead (*Citizen Kane*, "*Bewitched*", etc.). I did some acting under Gist and his version of the Stanislavski method and got technical film advice wherever I could find it. I later met the Brisbane animator Max Bannah, who gave me some tips and contacts for materials and remains a friend. But for the animation itself I was on my own, except for two books: *The Technique of Film Animation*[9] and *How to Animate Film Cartoons*.[10] The latter—by Preston Blair, a former Disney animator—was more helpful about the practical matter of making drawings move. For me, there was never any consideration of other traditional animation techniques such as stop motion and its use of the puppet tradition; they were simply outside my experience.

Then there was the matter of drawing itself. I had no previous art education and was new to life drawing, terms like "gouache" and "chiaroscuro", and everything else except newspaper and magazine cartoons. These were my influences, along with all the films and television I had ever seen, and now morning doses of *Sesame Street* animation. I had by now persuaded the Federal government's Experimental Film and Television Fund to give me, with nothing to offer but promises, $530 to make the film. Faced with the urgent matter of creating an animated film, and guided by the two books, I started the process by drawing designs and storyboards, just as they prescribed.

Now I had to decide: what exactly would *happen* in this film, and in what order? In this, fortunately, I was guided by the lyrics of the song which were specific enough to illustrate but also open to interpretation. In my cartoon *Please Don't Bury Me* all those angels in heaven—film stars gathered around the Paradise movie theatre topped with a huge ice cream cone—are gathered to report the last words of the newly deceased, and later to eat him. Between John's arrival and the feast we see my animated interpretations of lines in the song, as humorous and varied—and as simple to animate—as I could make them.

First John sees his own death on the big screen, as a replay in slow motion.

This recalls an early Émile Cohl animated farce (*Fantasmagorie*, 1908) with a chalk figure in a movie-within-a-movie, but also later Buster Keaton comedies and the slo-mo replay of "Slim" the gunfighter in my own *Dance of Death*.[11] Later we see John in the back of the hearse, sawing off the feet of his own corpse ("give my feet to the footloose") and then giving his knees "to the (k)needy".

We also see John's smelly sox put "in a cedar box, just get 'em out of here", the hearse being attacked by a Venus De Milo with John's cartoon arms holding a machine gun, and other scenes related to the lyrics. Some lines such as "Throw my brain in a hurricane/And the blind can have my eyes..." were part of the song's chorus and would be heard more than once. Having bought the rights to use the words and music in a new recording for the film, I was able to plan the timing of scenes to accommodate my plans for illustrating them. Without realizing it I was, by timing the music to the planned animation, already being more ambitious than making a video clip of an existing recording. And I was fortunate to have a talented musician (a fellow student, Dave Lemon) who was able to play guitar and sing in a one-take "live" recording without over-dubs or audio editing.

My first piece of filmed animation, and my first use of 16 mm film, was a test of the animation equipment I would use for *Please Don't Bury Me*: a borrowed Bolex camera bolted vertically onto a wall bracket, with a separate horizontal table below it for the artwork. Both were made from steel by my father. The test produced two very primitive films: one using cut-outs and inter-titles, the other drawn under the camera and reversed to play backwards. It was a technical success, though neither film was ever edited or finished with sound.

For *Please Don't Bury Me*, however, I had been paid $530 to make a real *cartoon*, with the animation process familiar from many childhood episodes of Walt Disney's television *Fantasyland: The Happiest Kingdom of Them All*, and as instructed by the two books. There would be many pencil drawings which had to be traced with ink onto sheets of acetate "cels". These were then painted and shot against illustrated backgrounds using the "professional" 16mm film format. In the pre-digital 1970s these were all physical media, with pools of wet paint on the cels, drying racks, and a laboratory to process the film. As instructed by the books, I also shot "pencil tests" of important drawn sequences. These were exciting to see when they came back from the laboratory: unforgettably, my drawings moved! (However rough and awkward the animation, they were never re-drawn.)

Despite the vigorous examples of Disney animation from the Preston Blair book, little of *Please Don't Bury Me* was drawn in a complicated way that would require testing. I was in a hurry to make a film, not to become a Disney animator; already the animated drawings were a means to an end. The simple animation spots on *Sesame Street* had taught me the dark arts of "limited animation": the use of repetition, pauses in action, and still artwork that moved under the camera. Very fast movements, like John's crash through the "Welcome" mat in Heaven, were accomplished with no animation at all: an instantaneous "jump cut" and a big sound in post-production to ease the jarring visual effect. More sophisticated cartoon animation effects, like drawn or painted blurs, were as yet outside my understanding or ability.

This was a visualization of a song, rather than an on-screen performance. Though I now knew Robert Gist's "method" approach to acting on the stage, I had no illusions about my ability to bring Stanislavski to the characters in my cartoon short.[12] There was also no lip-sync in the film, so I could postpone learning another craft skill: matching mouth shapes to vocal sounds or "lip-sync animation".

I had already begun careers in two professions (archivist and teacher) but had resigned from both. I had always been able to evade the issue of craft: being trained to do a certain thing in a certain way, usually with one's hands, and with generally predictable results. Both my father and brother had been apprentice boilermakers who studied and practised their metal-working craft alongside tradesmen until they qualified as tradesmen themselves. Before the development of art schools, artists served apprenticeships with masters, learning the crafts of painting and sculpture as assistants until they too became masters with their own studios and apprentices.

The professional animation studio was a development of this system, combined with the efficiency of a modern production line to produce a unique product: the film or television series. With the feature *Animal Farm* (1954) and many other productions behind him, the UK producer John Halas described the animation studio in 1971.

> Whatever the size of the unit, the work to be undertaken is fundamentally the same.... In the smaller units an artist or technician may fulfil more than one of these functions.
> The Producer
> The Director
> The Designer, Lay-Out Artist and Background Artist
> The Key Animator
> The Assistant Animator
> The Inker and Colourist
> The Checker
> The Cameraman
> The Editor
> The Studio Manager[13]

Many independent animators did most of these ten tasks or, as with *Please Don't Bury Me* and its $530 budget, all of them. With all the films under discussion here, using various 2D techniques over 45 years as a writer/director/producer, I have never done fewer than four. In this situation the distinction between "artist" and "technician" is necessarily blurred or absent. There is, on the one hand, a breakdown in the strict hierarchy of roles that afflicts many production processes—not least the large studios where many trained "artists", often dreaming of their unmade auteur works, find themselves in technical roles where only narrow craft skills are required. On the other hand, many small independent productions suffer from technical faults and lack of craft skills, the result of inadequate training, experience, and (often) money.

This is true of any film production and is not peculiar to animation. As the director John Boorman has said, film making is the tedious, highly technical, and expensive process of turning "money into light".[14] Live action cinematography, like photography, is essentially a medium that records the life of whatever is in front of the camera. It is still "the Kingdom of Shadows" of the Lumière cinématographe that Maxim Gorky reported seeing at the Nizhni-Novgorod fair in 1896.[15] But animation not only has to *make* its images—otherwise there is nothing to see on screen—but also to *move* them, to achieve "the illusion of life". The necessity for these tasks is reflected in the literature of craft skills that has grown up around animation and its many techniques: drawing with various materials, clay, cut-outs, silhouettes, pin-screen, abstraction, direct-to-film, pixillation, rotoscope and the rest, and of course all the varieties of computer animation which now dominate the field.

With his *Animated Cartoons* (1920) E.G. Lutz is the best-known of the early guides to cartoons: "How they are made, their origin and development".[16] He starts with the magic lantern, the thaumatrope, and other optical toys, and works through extremely detailed descriptions of both "natural" movement (from the sequential photographs of Eadweard Muybridge[17,18]) and how to draw action in animated cartoons. In Lutz's pre-Disney book there are many suggestions of labour-saving short cuts, but the subject of sound is not mentioned. The book ends with the promise of colour, still years away in 1920.[19] In 1951 John Halas began developing instructional books for the amateur[20]—still without advice on sound—and the professional animator.[21] In a chapter of the latter book many of the less conventional non-cartoon techniques are discussed, as well as the work of Norman McLaren and several "Future Animation Technologies". This chapter describes technologies such as the long-forgotten "animascope", "traceur d'ectoplasmes", and "animograph"—along with "computer animation" which *was*, of course, the future. Brian Salt contributes a section on "Mathematics in Aid of Animation". Salt was later to publish two books on the mathematical operation of the rostrum camera, another once-dominant technology now virtually obsolete.[22,23]

In the 1970s Lenny Lipton's *Independent Filmmaking* provided a remarkably detailed and ecumenical guide to the many techniques of 8 and 16 mm film-making. But the crafts of animation are given just two pages. "It's hard to start classifying types of animation, but not nearly as difficult as to explain what it is".[24] In a book with an introduction by Stan Brakhage this is surprising but not unusual. In their very different fields of film scholarship, and despite the enthusiasm of others like Eisenstein in his time,[25] both Deleuze (theory)[26,27] and Mast (comedy)[28] manage to ignore almost entirely the strange and varied world of animation. Happily, other writers have taken up the challenge. Along with the literature of animation generally—its history and particular genres, and monographs on particular film-makers—the books describing the range of animation techniques have grown in both size and scope, from Bob Godfrey's *Do-It-Yourself Animation Book* (1974),[29] Laybourne (1979),[30] Solomon and Stark (1983),[31] Noake (1988),[32] and Taylor (1996)[33] to Williams (2001),[34] Furniss (2008),[35] and Cotte (2018).[36] The continued necessity of these books emphasizes the (literal) creativity at the heart of animation, which makes something out of nothing: a moving image from an idea. They also make clear the vital role of craft and technique: the only way of doing so.

This has led to an inevitable tension between art and craft in the making of images that move. Paul Wells agrees with Preston Blair that, while animation is both an art and a craft, its many techniques and complicated processes mean that "it remains the case that animation is a craft-oriented process".[37] There is also an intricate relationship between the concerns and techniques of both animation and live action. As Wells points out in his detailed discussion of genre:

> Arguably, all animation works as a version of fine art in motion... a practice which is informed by generic "deep structures". These structures integrate and counterpoint form and meaning, and further, reconcile approach and application as the *essence* of the art. The generic outcomes of the animated film are imbued in its technical execution.[38]

The art of animation is often seen as a separate form of cinema defined by its creation "frame by frame" rather than in real time. The film-maker Pierre Hebert, who for many years has scratched directly onto film in live performance, takes issue with this definition, which "implicitly puts the trade of animation at its centre.... It is a definition more for animators than for directors and I think it is responsible for the general weakness of aesthetics in the field of animation".[39] For Hebert the central problem is that, though animation and live action share a common history, the claim to realism of the cinematic apparatus has put the two in very different positions. By hiding the apparatus of camera and sound, and copying the real world, live action has made its claim to realism. Although free of this restriction, "for the most part animation has been mimicking live action cinema. Where live action has based itself on the idea of realism, animation has based itself on fantasy".[40] But now Hebert sees the new technologies as dissolving the boundaries between all the technological arts, which potentially "above all makes the human body visible at the centre of the artistic activity even if it is of a technological nature".[41]

Whether described as technological, technical, or as craft, the means of artistic production have always been central to the arts. And as long as the artists are humans, and not machines, the artist's own very mortal mind and body—with their shared and inevitable fate—remains responsible for the use of those means. This is true for Hebert in his performance-based animation practice, but also for any animator toiling to create the "illusion of life" on a pin screen or a computer screen or in a virtual reality environment. And it is also true—as an "illusion of fate", we might call it—for the cartoon avatar of John Prine in *Please Don't Bury Me* who wakes up in his "mortal" body, puts on his slippers, walks into the kitchen and dies.

At the end of his book's extensive technical section, written a century ago, Lutz describes the moment of completion for the film maker, who is evidently independent and working alone: "Then only will the artist be able to see, as a finality, his skill as an animator, his expertness as a technical worker, his cleverness as a humorist, and the extent of his adroitness in plot construction".[42] There follows "Canine Thoughts", a comic strip of a dog looking at a dish and thinking of a bone. "In giving screen life to the above, the dog and dish would be drawn but once on celluloid and the other parts separately drawn for each phase of the movement".[43] One of the "other parts" is a dotted line going straight from the dog's eye to the dish, indicating the direction of the animated eyeline and the dog's one thought: food.

Working alone in Toowoomba in 1976, and without Lutz to guide me, I came up with the same solution to the same problem as John wakes up and looks at his alarm clock: how to show a character's thoughts.

Lacking a ruler, however, my dotted line is drawn freehand as an animated wobble. John yawns and we see his legs lumber badly, like tree-stumps, towards the door—and his death. John's reaction to the fatal event is rendered as two eyeballs peering around at the darkness, first in confusion and then desperation, and in total silence. Eventually the eyeballs join in sadness as a blue tear runs down between them and drops out of frame. Still in his pyjamas, John now hurtles out of the darkness to hit the screen.

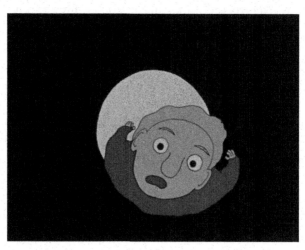

Only now does the song resume. "And oh, what a feeling!/ When my soul went through the ceiling…".

John is now in heaven but sadly, after 30 seconds of stony silence in the eyeball scene, the film's sound has not improved. A clean music recording had somehow become a muddy 16 mm film soundtrack. After complaints to the laboratory, a final print was sent to me with a new title on the can: *Please **Bury** Me.* As a novice I had no answer to this unkind suggestion from a "professional" laboratory. It only reminded me of the film's other deficiencies in craft: the uneven "flickering" exposure of the clockwork 16 mm camera, the often awkward animation, my beginner's uncertainty of timing and cutting. By now I was committed to making more and better films and went to film school in Melbourne to learn the necessary craft skills. First, though, I took the professionals' "advice" and buried the film in a box. It was unseen for decades.

NOTES

1 Prine, John. *Sweet Revenge.* Atlantic Records, 1973.
2 Agee, James and Walker Evans. *Let Us Now Praise Famous Men.* Boston: Houghton Mifflin, 1969.
3 White, Patrick. *The Tree of Man.* London: Penguin, 1963.
4 Swift, Jonathan. *A Modest Proposal.* https://www.gutenberg.org/ files/1080/1080-h/1080-h.htm Accessed 5-2-20.
5 https://simple.wikipedia.org/wiki/Massa%27s_in_de_Cold_ Ground#cite_note-FOOTNOTEEmerson200-1 Retrieved 5-2-20.
6 https://www.youtube.com/watch?v=EfPHpb2U9go.
7 Huffman, Eddie quoted in https://www.telegraph.co.uk/culture/ music/worldfolkandjazz/11464892/John-Prine-biography-review. html Retrieved 10-11-19.
8 https://en.wikipedia.org/wiki/Robert_Gist.
9 Halas, John and Roger Manvell. *The Technique of Film Animation.* London and New York: Focal Press, 1971.
10 Blair, Preston. *How to Animate Film Cartoons.* Tustin, CA: Walter T. Foster, 1980.
11 Bermel, Alfred. *Farce.* New York: Touchstone, 1982. 226.

12 Honess Roe, Annabelle. "Animation and Performance" in: Dobson, Nichola, Annabelle Honess Roe, Amy Ratelle and Caroline Ruddell (eds). *The Animation Studies Reader*. New York, London: Bloomsbury Academic, 2020. 74–75.

13 Halas and Manvell, op. cit. 210.

14 Boorman, John. *Money Into Light: A Diary*. London: Faber & Faber, 1985.

15 Adair, Gilbert (ed.) op. cit. 10–13.

16 Lutz, E.G. *Animated Cartoons: How They Are Made, Their Origin and Development*. New York: Charles Scribner's Sons, 1920. 219.

17 Muybridge, Eadweard. *Animals in Motion*. New York: Dover, 1957.

18 Muybridge, Eadweard. *The Human Figure in Motion*. New York: Dover, 1955.

19 Lutz. op. cit. 260–261.

20 Halas, John and Bob Privett. *How to Cartoon for Amateur Films*. London and New York: Focal Press, 1958 (3rd ed.).

21 Halas, John and Roger Manvell. *The Technique of Film Animation*. London and New York: Focal Press, 1971 (3rd ed.).

22 Salt, Brian G.D. *Movements in Animation (Vol. I)*. Oxford: Pergamon. 1976.

23 Salt, Brian G.D. *Programmes for Animation*. Oxford: Pergamon. 1976.

24 Lipton, Lenny. *Independent Filmmaking*. San Francisco: Straight Arrow Books, 1972. 197–198.

25 Leyda, Jay (ed.) *Eisenstein on Disney*. London: Methuen, 1988.

26 Deleuze, Gilles. *Cinema 1: The Movement-Image*. Minneapolis: University of Minneapolis Press, 1986.

27 Deleuze, Gilles. *Cinema 2: The Time-Image*. Minneapolis: University of Minneapolis Press, 1989.

28 Mast, Gerald. *The Comic Mind: Comedy and the Movies*. Chicago: University of Chicago Press, 1979.

29 Godfrey, Bob and Anna Jackson. *The Do-It-Yourself Animation Book*. London: BBC Publications, 1974.

30 Laybourne, Kit. *The Animation Book*. New York: Crown Publishers, 1979.

31 Solomon, Charles and Ron Stark. *The Complete Kodak Animation Book*. Rochester, NY: Eastman Kodak, 1983.

32 Noake, Roger. *Animation: A Guide to Animated Film Techniques*. London: Macdonald Orbis, 1988.

33 Taylor, Richard. *The Encyclopedia of Animation Techniques*. East Roseville, NSW: Simon and Schuster, 1996.

34 Williams, Richard. *The Animator's Survival Kit*. London and New York: Faber and Faber, 2001.
35 Furniss, Maureen. *The Animation Bible: A Guide to Everything – From Flipbooks to Flash*. London: Lawrence King Publishing, 2008.
36 Cotte, Olivier. *Le Grand Livre des Techniques du Cinéma du'Animation*. Paris: Dunod, 2018.
37 Wells, Paul. *Animation: Genre and Authorship*. London: Wallflower, 2002. 66.
38 ibid. 66 (italics in original).
39 Hebert, Pierre. "Cinema, Animation, and the Other Arts: An Unanswered Question" in: Gehman, Chris and Steve Reinke (eds). *The Sharpest Point: Animation at the End of Cinema*. Toronto: YVZ Books, 2005. 182.
40 ibid. 184.
41 ibid. 186.
42 Lutz. op. cit. 219.
43 ibid. 219.

CHAPTER 3

Dance of Death (1983)

Because I could not stop for Death –
He kindly stopped for me –

EMILY DICKINSON (C1862)[1]

After completing *Please Don't Bury Me*, and then the 1-year animation course at Swinburne in 1977, I set myself up in Melbourne as a freelance animator. With a 16 mm camera on a new rostrum made by my father in Brisbane, I could shoot my own animation as well as titles and animation for other people. Gradually I began to get commissions for graphics and television commercials, if necessary shot elsewhere on a rented 35 mm rostrum.

One job in 1978 was the design and animation of the title and credits sequences for *STAX* (1979), an ambitious new children's television programme for commercial television, to be made as an independent production (The jingle went: "We've got stacks of these and stacks of those and stacks of that..."). I was also asked to write and animate very short visual jokes to act as interstitials between the live action segments of the loosely formatted programme. These were submitted to the producer by phone (both idea and price), discussed and commissioned on the spot, and delivered as mute animation soon after. For economy's sake I

DOI: 10.1201/9781003199663-3

used as many animation tricks as I knew—creating extra gags by having several pay-offs from one set-up, simple graphics and animated cycles, sudden movement after dramatic pauses— anything to make animated comedy that was visually interesting, funny, and very cheap to make. Almost miraculously, these "spots" were also to be free of dialogue (the curse of much television then and now), so the rhythms and pacing were cinematic rather than verbal or theatrical. These spots were very enjoyable to create, and I found I had the necessary facility for invention. They were, however, for children.

I was familiar with stranger and much darker images and humour from Europe[2,3,4,5] and the American underground "comix,"[6,7] as well as the great and continuing tradition of Australian cartoons, especially in daily newspapers like *The Age* in Melbourne with its roster of brilliant cartoonists.[8,9,10] The cartoonist and film maker Bruce Petty, after making several other animated films for adults including *Australian History* (1971), had recently won an Oscar for his animated short *Leisure* (1976).[11]

With the *STAX* spots in mind, I began to make up similar material for adults—though it was death and violence rather than sex that made the jokes "adult". There was no television outlet for this material, but television itself would provide both the subject and the structure for *Dance of Death* (1983).

At first, I was simply trying to come up with short visual jokes about death and violence. Some were scribbled down in a few words ("execution: interview with hanging man"); others were roughly storyboarded. There was a lot of junk to be thrown away as insufficiently violent or tele-visual, or simply not funny. I realized that changing channels would allow easy transitions that were both "violent" (sudden and graphic) and essential to the television experience: a "dance of death" in itself. Any sequence—or the whole film—could start at any point. As long as the jokes were entertaining, like television itself, the audience would soon figure it out.

But what was "it" exactly? What was the narrative? Was an overall narrative even necessary for this short film? After all, television was the home of sketch comedy and *Laugh-In* jokes as well as the sitcom. It was also cinematic as well as theatrical; I had by now seen many abstract and experimental non-narrative films, and had made one myself. My Swinburne student film *Jack Fig* (1977) had no images at all, just various colours dissolving at different rates in a blank colour-field as a subjective response to a guitar piece. But as a storyteller I wanted to combine the wild potential and sudden timing of my brief death-oriented spots with a story and human characters. For example: someone (or something) had to change the TV channels. If the film were to be engaging as drama, this person should be someone in the story.

Thinking of the typical *STAX* audience member—but with no thought of a family "G" rating for the film—I cast "little Sally Roberts" as a young girl with a remote control, hunting down the most violent moments she can find: the visual gags I devised for the film.

Sally is a connoisseur of television violence; she can mouth the words of familiar segments as they are announced ("later in the show: This Is Your Death, the segment I *know* you're all just *dying* to be in!"). Sally is annoyed only when called away for dinner.

Most of the gags are very simple. A reporter "interviews" a black child dying mutely of hunger (after dropping the dead child, the reporter signs off with a very BBC-style "David Robb. Africa"); a circus elephant accidentally flattens its trainer. In sports news, a weightlifter makes a successful lift but then crashes through the floor; a water-skier slams into a post; a diver splats into an empty swimming pool just as Sally's mother says "dinner".

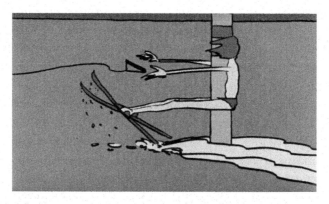

The most complicated visual gag is in several stages and starts the film. In the set-up, a pram is parked on a railway track (Cue: rolling silent-movie piano.).

The train approaches; the mother runs to save her baby. She gets there just in time to push the pram clear, but is splattered by the train across the screen. The pram then rattles towards a high cliff in silhouette and goes over the edge. The baby's death is unseen but heard as a dreadful crash. We are introduced to Sally as she titters with glee. But who is behind all this? Who has an interest in creating such carnage on television, and is powerful enough to pull it off? The Godless answer came from within.

The human skeleton is one of the oldest symbols of death and is found in many cultures.[12] There is no escaping its reality—we have one inside each of us, animated by muscle and will—nor its corollary, the shape of our individual narratives from birth to death. Yet one's own skeleton is necessarily an abstraction: something one can only imagine, particularly in movement. There is a natural pairing of the body and its skeleton: the living and the dead. The symbolic meeting of the two, taking place as a unique event at the end of each human life, has often been expressed as a "dance of death". Death (the skeleton) is usually seen as the great leveller, taking rich and poor, old and young, the great and the insignificant. And often this common approach has a religious dimension, assuring all believers that God's plan is carried out in its own spiritually democratic way.

I already knew Holbein's *Dance of Death*,[13] and would soon come to know Posada's *calaveras* from Mexico,[14] Rowlandson's *English Dance of Death*,[15] and many others, including the work of modern illustrators like Tomi Ungerer.[16] One of the most powerful influences for me was *Kubin's Dance of Death*,[17] a suite of drawings by the Austrian Alfred Kubin (1877–1959) which avoids both the moral tone of other artists and the requirements of religion. Kubin has a savage drawn line to match his uniquely disturbing and varied images. There was also the animated *The Skeleton Dance* ("a Walt Disney comic, drawn by Ub Iwerks", 1929) in which a group of skeletons strut their musical stuff in a gothic graveyard scene complete with owls, ghosts, and frightened animals, but with neither people nor any real terror.

I also knew well the famous final sequence in *The Seventh Seal* (Bergman, 1957) where a non-skeletal Death—pale, hooded, berobed, and wielding a scythe—leads a line of characters dancing along a hilltop, silhouetted against the evening sky. This was of course a live action film, with cinematography's necessarily direct presentation of life itself. But I was determined that there would be no live action or photographic images in *Dance of Death*. Whatever animation's claims to being "the illusion of life", this film about death would be 100% animation, without any images of actual mortals. It would be 100% *dead*. Equally, whatever the film's absurdities, exaggerations, and cartoon conventions, there would be no anthropomorphism, cartoon survivals, or resurrections for the characters. The film's animation is hand-drawn but deadly serious; as in life, the deaths in *Dance of Death* are permanent.

I wanted my skeletal Death to be a distinct character, not just one of a group of anonymous and identical human skeletons as in the Disney film, and to be directly identified with both television and modern life.

AN ANIMATED FILM BY DENNIS TUPICOFF

The ideal model was available here in Australia—and with an American accent. Known sometimes as "the lanky Yank", the entertainer Don Lane (1933–2009) hosted his "Tonight"-style variety programme on national television from 1975 to 1983. Morton Isaacson (his real name) was a sometime nightclub singer and comic who also interviewed special guests and had a "wheel of fortune" with prizes for contestants from the studio audience. For my purposes, all the skeletal Don Lane needed was a very skinny black suit, a red bow tie, and a new name announced as "the smiling skull: Don Death!"

The open format of Don Death's TV show "Dance of Death" lends itself to such inventions as a talent quest with judges who give points for the best violent death. Not everyone plays ball, of course; despite "that gorgeous spurt of blood" in the slo-mo replay of a talent-quest gunfight, Slim and Kitty score only 7 out of 10 from the three judges ("No last words for us", the Scots judge complains).

Slim's glamorous partner Kitty is left to sob, embracing the two halves of Slim's corpse. The show goes on, of course, for Don Death and for everyone else: "Not bad, not bad at all. Let's hear it for Slim and Kitty!"

Soon the lucky wheel spins. "Last week, if you remember, it was Poison!" For one lucky audience member (a delighted and self-introduced "Bill Stokes from Brighton") the "shocking" prize for a wheel-spin is his on-screen death by electrocution: "live" in the studio. And it's not quite instant: Bill gets to blurt out "a cheerio to my Mum…" before he sizzles in blue flashes. Beaming up at the studio monitors, the rest of the audience applaud and cheer as one. They ignore the blackened body of Bill Stokes, still sitting in their midst.

This studio audience in *Dance of Death* is a metaphorical representation of mass culture, lively and anonymous, and is animated as such.

Its 200 separate characters are all individual in size, age, dress, and colour. But they are identical in their cartoon roles and expressions: always smiling and applauding. (When things briefly turn sour during Mrs Roberts' attempt to stop proceedings, a different "boo!" cycle was used for the audience.) In animation terms this meant drawing 200 different characters as one drawing, and tracing it three times so that all the characters would vibrate with excitement onscreen: a "random cycle" of three cels. Each of the 200 audience members also had a pair of hands which were animated in an "applause cycle" of four drawings coming together and parting in a relentless rhythm, with each of the four phases of movement spread randomly across the field of smiling figures. This provided a lively array of mass audience, each applauding individually, which could be used as a static shot, panned across or zoomed in/out as required. Physically, the artwork for this shot still exists as one large framed image behind glass, with three long rows of applauding and anonymous cartoon characters. The fourth cel in the "applause cycle" survives as a disembodied set of hands in a separate row, below the others. Bill Stokes' place in this vast array is of course now blank. Bill is a separate drawing; he is an expendable member of the smiling throng—and he will not be coming back.

The show's highlight and finale each week is "This Is Your Death", an obvious inversion of the popular programme *This Is Your Life* which ran on television for many years. Family, friends, and associates would show up to pay tribute to that week's special guest. In this segment of "Dance of Death", a family of Don Death's fans is selected for their own personal (surprise) death. And tonight it's the Roberts family, whose young Sally has been featured throughout the film as an avid fan of television violence and particularly Don's "Dance of Death" show. When they are revealed as the chosen ones for "This Is Your Death", the Roberts' colours switch suddenly from pastels and grey to vibrant brightness. Sally is thrilled.

Both she and her father are deeply ashamed when her mum Mary tries to save the family, bashing fruitlessly at the remote control to change the channel, to turn the thing off—anything to stop the inevitable. But nothing has been left to chance; the remote control is now useless. As the studio audience boos Mrs Roberts' lapse in taste, Don Death orders a live cross to the extended "Roberts" family: young and old and infirm, smiling and waving under a "Roberts" family banner. Resigned now to her fate, Mary Roberts retreats in terror to join her frowning husband and daughter. While the audience starts a countdown ("10-9-8-7...") Sally begins a thank-you speech, but Don's patter has priority. The audience's countdown takes us up to the moment of "zero", when the house is flattened by a giant tombstone.

The three smiling Roberts faces have already been carved into the marble, ready for their monumental afterlife.

Don Death ends the show with an invitation to his "very special guest" and lucky wheel assistant, an elderly fan from Surrey Hills called Ada Fern.

Don: And now: shall we dance, Ada?

Ada: Oh yes, Don! And thank you so much! For everything!

As they dance, Don remembers meeting Ada's late husband Ron: "Cancer, wasn't it?" Ada is radiant; but she is not likely to see another bingo night.

In animating the final dance of Ada with Don, I used a diagram from a dance instruction book. These diagrams show the floor positions for each partner as graphic feet, and the direction of each foot's movement as a dotted line. The piano music for this sequence had already been recorded: the classic "death march" but played by Peter Sullivan in 3/4 "waltz" time. The animation was drawn as a cycle that matched that rhythm, but also followed the necessarily rather mechanical steps of such a dance, as analysed in the diagram. As they move against a white limbo background, apparently in a swirling circular motion, Ada and Don are obviously animated drawings. But they "really" dance to this music in an appropriate waltz.

By now there is no more changing of channels. Death is in control. (Of course—as Don Death would claim and tradition would agree—Death is *always* in control.) The credits roll over an evening suburban landscape filled with bright living rooms and TV aerials silhouetted against the night sky. The huge Roberts headstone is spot-lit; the music vamps; the audience cheers.

Dance of Death is structured as a trap, with gags as the bait. And wherever the film has been screened, audience reactions have been remarkably similar. At first viewers are amused and engaged at the outrageous action: after all, it's only a cartoon. The constant changes of scene and programme style (from sports to news, variety to circus) are acceptable and entertaining as long as the comedy keeps coming. But as the body count rises, as the animated studio audience grows ever more enthusiastic, and as the Roberts family becomes more involved, the laughter subsides. Entertainment is replaced by discomfort; the film's audience is by now implicated in a dance of death of its own.

*

The original publicity synopsis for *Dance of Death* was:

> To the long tradition of the human skeleton in art and folklore, *Dance of Death* brings the new context of mass media—and television violence. In fact, for thrill-seeking Sally Roberts, faced with a welter of variety, sports, and

> news programmes, changing TV channels itself becomes
> a dance of death. "Television violence: where will it end?"
> *Dance of Death* asks this question. Plays with it, laughs
> with it, thrills to it. Hacks it to pieces.

Though the intentions of the film are both comic and serious, this description deliberately avoids the term "satire". In his study of satire, Arthur Pollard says bluntly: "Satire always has a victim, it always criticizes."[18] Earlier he suggests that "love and death are in their essential magnificence beyond the reach of satire. In comedy or tragedy, they may be celebrated and exalted. Satire does not exalt; it deflates..."[19]

By invoking the tradition of the dance of death, this short film steps back from a satirical attack (however justified) on the prevalence of television violence. It intends to be entertaining, darkly humorous and to make a strongly cinematic comment on human nature and television, as Neil Postman was to do so powerfully, in a different way, in his book *Amusing Ourselves to Death*[20] (itself following Jerry Mander's provocatively titled *Four Arguments for the Elimination of Television*[21]). *Dance of Death* was released in 1983, in a more innocent era, before the internet made almost everything accessible, and before "reality television". Many of the images I imagined as exaggerated animation have by now been on television as real news or entertainment, or are available on-line any time as real images, real deaths of real human beings.

There have been many animated films set largely in the world of death and skeletons.[22] *Tim Burton's The Nightmare Before Christmas* (Selick, 1993) stars a skeleton ("Jack Skellington") and is almost wholly concerned with the grotesque and highly musical characters in the animated world designed by Burton. There is very little crossover between the living and the dead. (Despite its dark theme and scenes of torture and violence, *Nightmare* shares with *Dance of Death* the peculiarity of a "G" rating—surely evidence that the censor sees animation as harmless, whatever its subject and treatment.) The film ends on a moonlight kiss between Jack and Sally, the romantic interest. But both are of the Dead; they are not going anywhere, especially to the land of the Living.

Pixar/Disney's *Coco* (Unkrich, Molina, 2017) is set during the Day of the Dead in Mexico, "when our ancestors visit us". With its determinedly parallel worlds, the film is finally a family tale of ambition, treachery, discovery, and redemption from beyond the grave. These dead people, although skeletal, are not yet *finally* dead; The Final Death, we are told, takes place only when one is forgotten by the Living. And here there is a nod to the Photograph. Amongst the lavish Pixar animation there is ingenious use of "photographs" and "old films"—*non-photographic* illustrations animated with CGI, so without reality outside *Coco*—as markers of both the past and the soul. One "photograph" is first unfolded to reveal a man with one corner (his head) torn off; much later the torn corner is found and re-attached as the character's true identity is established and the story is resolved.

A literary work set on the Day of the Dead in Mexico is Malcolm Lowry's hell-haunted and mescal-soaked novel *Under the Volcano*, in which the alcoholic Consul staggers from one drink to another in a succession of bars, towards his inevitable and violent death.[23] John Huston's 1984 live action adaptation avoids the Consul's hallucinations entirely, relying instead on attractive but conventional art direction and cinematography, and Albert Finney's remarkable performance. The film fails to turn the language of the novel and its visions of the Consul's personal Hell—which was also Lowry's—into a cinematic reality.[24] And unlike *Coco* there can be no affirmative, resolved, happy ending for the Consul. He is shot several times by some local gangsters and his body is kicked into a ravine. His last words in the film are: "What a dingy way to die".

Coco is anything but dingy. It is bright and spectacularly animated, crowded with people and affecting situations in the worlds of both life and death. But sadly the Consul's alcoholic visions in *Under the Volcano* are never likely to be animated by Pixar; the sordid details of one man's Hell are probably not on the Disney agenda. I once asked a Pixar features director whether really adult material was—like other films made for adults—ever likely to come from a large and successful animation studio like Pixar. His irritated reply was: "Dennis, do you know how much these movies *cost*?" In fact there is a crucial murder in *Coco*, but it is not shown in any detail. It seems to be merely a necessity of plot as the last strands of the story come together.

Catherine Russell begins her book *Narrative Mortality* by quoting Roland Barthes on Death and Photography[25] (a subject to be discussed later). She goes on: "Death remains feared, denied, and hidden, and yet images of death are a staple of the mass media."[26] Later she says that death can be represented in two ways on film: by "actual documented death" and "by an actor pretending to die".[27]

Animation does not, of course, normally look like life (or death) except when used as special effects in live action. But as used in *Dance of Death*—a serious cartoon using comic elements without ever aiming for realism—animation can be regarded as a third way to represent death on film, beside the actual and the enacted live action. "The prevalence of violent death in the mass media is… attributable to the demands of the medium: speed and spectacle, but also to the melodramatic desire to 'see the unseeable'."[28] Even when stripped of melodrama and violence, the rendering of the invisible has always been one of animation's great strengths. Too small, too big, too far, too dangerous, too complex, too abstract, too bloody, too dark, too light, or simply because the event happened too long ago, or was not filmed in the first place; for all these reasons and more, animation has often been used to illustrate and clarify what would otherwise remain obscure or hidden altogether. With its powerful ability to present imaginatively what is unseen, animation has a special ability to portray television violence.

In a section called "Dances of Death", Russell discusses the death-scene "ballets" of two Hollywood films: *Bonnie and Clyde*

(Penn, 1967) and *The Wild Bunch* (Peckinpah, 1969). As director, Arthur Penn is very specific about his requirements: "I wanted two kinds of death: Clyde's to be rather like a ballet, and Bonnie's to have the physical shock."[29] He claims to be aiming for a "mythical, legendary, balletic ending."[30]

> One of the conventions by which the gruesomeness of (violent) death is 'contained' in narrative is slow motion, also a key means by which violence can be construed as ballet.... (A)lthough slow motion is 'less real' than twenty-four frames per second, when used to depict death, it achieves a degree of realism.[31]

In discussing a "choreography of dying", Russell moves on to the *danse macabre* (dance of death) and to Philippe Aries and his great book *The Hour of Our Death*.[32] But in doing so she misses two important points. First: the classic dance of death is not a solo and sometimes acrobatic performance like the slow-motion death by gunfire, but a *pas de deux*. The (usually skeletal) figure of Death leads the dance with the (newly deceased) partner. Second: the entirely symbolic dance of death in its traditional form, as described by Aries in *The Hour of Our Death*[33] and illustrated in his *Images of Man and Death*,[34] requires a graphic or plastic expression. It does not lend itself well to photography or live action cinema. In that sense, animation is the most appropriate way to update the dance of death.

In his book *Animations of Mortality* the "Monty Python" animator and later live action director Terry Gilliam also employs the ballet metaphor. He explains his preference for the much quicker and cheaper cut-out technique, rather than "ordinary" (drawn) animation. "Admittedly, the (drawn) movements are elaborate and graceful—but who needs it? If that's what the public wants they can go to the ballet."[35]

As a film maker my interest in skeletons and death has continued. Since completing *Dance of Death* in 1983 I have written two (mostly live action) feature films set in the territory between

Life and Death. One stars an animated skeleton who has joined the Dead willingly enough via suicide, but has a unique chance to regain life. In the other, a live action animator ("Ralph") meets his Death, a portly and mostly affable character ("Sam") who occasionally becomes a fearsome skeletal antagonist. (Their names come from the Chuck Jones characters who clock on and off their roles in his "Wolf and Sheep Dog" shorts, 1953–1963.) Unhappy about dying, Ralph tells animated stories as a delaying tactic—the Scheherazade method—but Sam replies in kind. As the live action story develops and follows their animated stories, it also follows the five progressive stages of Ralph's dying, as described by Elisabeth Kübler-Ross: denial, anger, bargaining, depression, acceptance.[36] Unproduced, both films exist only in the abstracted, ghostly forms of screenplays and storyboards. They wait, as the Coyote's Acme devices wait for water in the "Coyote and Roadrunner" cartoons (Jones, 1949–1965), for money to be added. But life and death go on.

*

The model for Don Death, Don Lane, died in 2009. But his *Don Lane Show* co-host Bert Newton (1938-2021) was still occasionally active until the year of his death. In about 1995 he interviewed me on his national TV programme *Good Morning Australia*, to talk about the imminent theatrical release of my short *The Darra Dogs*. But the reality of live TV was far from the animated excitement and mayhem of *Dance of Death*.

The studio "audience" were just the few technicians on the floor that weekday morning. Newton himself was slumped on the couch, almost inert until the red "On Air" light came on. Suddenly he came to life as my interviewer, though he showed no sign of having seen any of my films, including *The Darra Dogs*. At the end he rose and, without warning, insisted on my standing beside him to show my full height (2.1 m/6′10″), to scattered laughs and applause from the crew. The red "On Air" light then went off. Newton slumped back onto the couch. I was free to go.

NOTES

1 Franklin, R.W. (ed). *The Poems of Emily Dickinson*. Cambridge, MA: Belknap Press, 1999. 219.
2 Lucie-Smith, Edward. *The Waking Dream: Fantasy and the Surreal in Graphic Art 1450-1900*. New York: Knopf, 1975.
3 Steadman, Ralph. *Between the Eyes*. London: Jonathan Cape, 1984.
4 Topor, Roland. *Dessins*. Paris: Albin Michel, 1968.
5 Wright, Thomas. *A History of Caricature and Grotesque in Literature and Art [1865]*. New York: Ungar, 1968.
6 Lestren, Mark James. *A History of Underground Comics*. San Francisco, CA: Straight Arrow Books, 1974.
7 Lynch, Jay. *The Best of Bijou Funnies*. London: Omnibus, 1975.
8 Hutchinson, Garrie (ed.) *The Awful Australian*. South Yarra: Curry O'Neil Ross, 1984.
9 King, Jonathan. *Stop Laughing, This Is Serious!* Stanmore, NSW: Cassell Australia, 1978.
10 Pinder, Phil. (writer/editor). *Down Underground Comix*. Ringwood: Penguin, 1983.
11 Petty, Bruce. *Petty's Australia – And How It Works*. Ringwood: Penguin, 1976.
12 https://en.wikipedia.org/wiki/Death_(personification).
13 Holbein, Hans the Younger. *The Dance of Death*. New York: Dover, 1971
14 Rothenstein, Julian (ed). *J.G Posada: Messenger of Mortality*. London: Redstone Press, 1989.
15 Rowlandson, Thomas and: "Doctor Syntax". *The English Dance of Death Vols. 1&2*. London: Methuen, 1903.
16 Ungerer, Tomi. *The Underground Sketchbook of Tomi Ungerer*. New York: Dover, 1964.
17 Kubin, Alfred. *Kubin's Dance of Death and Other Drawings*. New York: Dover, 1973.
18 Pollard, Arthur. *Satire*. London: Methuen, 1970. 73.
19 ibid 7.
20 Postman, Neil. *Amusing Ourselves to Death*. London: Methuen, 1987.
21 Mander, Jerry. *Four Arguments for the Elimination of Television*. New York: William Morrow, 1978.
22 *Other films treat death variously as subject, e.g.: Corpse Bride (Burton & Johnson, 2005), Death and the Mother (Lingford, 1997); Rejected (Hertzfeldt, 2000); Sunday (Moyes, 1992).*
23 Lowry, Malcolm. *Under the Volcano*. London: Jonathan Cape, 1947.

24 Day, Douglas. *Malcolm Lowry: A Biography.* New York: Oxford University Press, 1974.
25 Russell, Catherine. *Narrative Mortality.* Minneapolis: University of Minnesota Press, 1995.
26 ibid. 1.
27 ibid. 70.
28 ibid. 75.
29 Quoted, ibid. 178.
30 Quoted, ibid. 182.
31 ibid. 186.
32 ibid. 187–188.
33 Aries, Philippe. The Hour of Our Death. London: Allen Lane, 1981.
34 Aries, Philippe. *Images of Man and Death.* Cambridge, MA: Harvard University Press. 1985.
35 Gilliam, Terry. *Animations of Mortality.* London: Eyre Methuen, 1978.
36 Kübler-Ross, Elisabeth. *On Death and Dying.* London: Tavistock, 1970.

CHAPTER 4

The Heat, The Humidity (1999)

"It's not the heat, it's the humidity."

—*common saying (Queensland)*

Until 1998 all my personal non-commercial films had been funded by the national Australian Film Commission.[1] Now there was a call for submissions by a three-way coalition of the AFC, several state film bodies, and (critically) the production arm of a national broadcaster: SBS Independent. The call for submissions for the *Swimming Outside the Flags* anthology series was brief and open; the films were to be short and animated, with a limited budget, and were to be packaged for television into half-hour programmes, each with several films. Although I had made cartoons for TV commercials, children's television, and educational films, it had been 15 years since I had written and animated a humorous cartoon of my own—*Dance of Death* in 1983. This was a chance to make a funny film for adults, and on broadcast television.

DOI: 10.1201/9781003199663-4

The idea for *The Heat, The Humidity* came from my home state of Queensland and its coastal climate. Generally subtropical in the south and tropical in the north, hot weather was very common and, especially in the summer, exacerbated by the "stickiness" of high humidity. Observations or complaints about the heat were often met with a sentence of explanation and elaboration, an idiomatic declaration of the true source of the sweaty weather: "It's not the heat, it's the humidity". This statement had become so common and so worn that it was a cliché, but one that was faintly amusing, if only for the many situations in which it was used by so many people. (It was said that in a bigger city like Sydney one could make a similar, more social complaint at times of discomfort: "It's not the heat, it's the humanity".)

I knew I would be working with the digital tools by now commonplace in commercial production. The low budget meant that the animation had to be quite simple. This became an interesting problem: just how simple could this film be? Why not make it in black-and-white? Could that same sentence ("It's not the heat, it's the humidity".) be repeated many times in different situations? Could it be the *only* piece of dialogue? And if the aim was to make a minimal cartoon with that one line of laconic Queensland talk, who should say it? This cartoon needed a leading character, a hero. Or, because it was a cartoon, an anti-hero. "Who should say it?" was perhaps the wrong question. Many situations suggested many speakers and one (mute) listener. Hence came the idea of a cartoon featuring a bank robber constantly being told the same thing: "It's not the heat. It's the humidity".

Looking at "cartoon narrative" in both animated and live action films, Brian Henderson reflects on the use of both ellipsis and repetition for comic purposes. In the simplified world of animation, the short cuts of ellipsis can be very rapid; in a cartoon short, they often need to be. "(C)artoon narratives proceed by repeating a basic situation with variations rather than by moving progressively toward a narrative resolution".[2] This often happens despite continuing failure—the cycle of endless failure, one might say—as with Elmer Fudd's pursuit of Bugs Bunny.[3] In his extensive discussion of cycles in animation, Dan Torre examines the peculiar affinity between animation and the repetition of action: "A cycle can be thought of as a type of dialectic, for even though it repeats, it also pushes forward".[4] Despite his account of cycles in the physical world as well as in animation, Torre is careful to emphasize that "time is always experienced in a linear manner—actions may be repeated (or more precisely re-enacted), but not *time*".[5] Life really does move on. And, for the bank robber in *The Heat, The Humidity*, all the narrative repetition and animation cycles do not make him an Elmer Fudd or a Coyote. As in life, they move him rapidly towards not only the narrative resolution of death, but also physical decline and annihilation.

Until now, most of my films were fractured in time and place. They had often been based on memories or imagined stories that had no relation to the unfolding passage of time, and were often deliberately edited at the storyboard stage to create unease and surprise. Even with Kathy Easdale's very chronological narrative in *His Mother's Voice* (see Chapter 7), the apparently continuous one-shot action of Part 2 follows the same story told in many shots and several locations in Part 1. *The Heat, The Humidity* is very short and its structure is very simple. It has a beginning, a middle, and an end (in that order) and a central character whose progress is from airport arrival to mortal "departure", from rude health to physical dissolution.

By now I had made two animated films about real events that could be termed "documentaries" (see Chapters 6 and 7). But this was to be a *cartoon*, a graphic fiction free to exaggerate and be silly. I already had a very clear image of my bank robber: a standard cartoon character who is chunky, bald, armed with a pistol and (of course) always wears a robber's eye-mask.

As noted by a boy on the plane, the felon's recent escape from jail is front-page news. He quickly and violently shuts down the boy's scream of alarm, and stares out of the window with relish as the plane lands in the "Gateway to the Tropics".

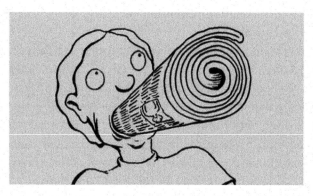

His profession and attitude is very clear by now; there is no need for this determined, sturdy, and well-dressed thug to say anything. But as soon as he leaves the plane he bursts into a sweat, then collapses in a faint. Flat on the tarmac, already gasping, he wakes to hear these words from one of the bystanders silhouetted above him, and with a country twang: "It's not the heat, it's the humidity".

The hot and sultry Queensland weather is often likened to a sweat-box or a sauna. (Waiting on a cab rank in my non-air-conditioned taxi in the 1970s, I watched the sweat ooze from my pores, and felt the shirt stick to my skin.). Now the possibilities of the cartoon form opened up. Wanting only to ply his trade, the robber sheds great graphic drops of sweat, loses layers of clothes, and shrinks visibly.

His desperate and worsening situation is exacerbated by a succession of friendly Queenslanders who say only and inevitably: "It's not the heat, it's the humidity". If he is disturbed they are calm; if he is sweaty and afraid they are dry and reassuring. The cartoon, like the robber's attempts to get rich by robbing a bank, becomes a farce.

Now I could add the unique properties of animation, possible even in a low-budget black and white cartoon. In a world of humidity there could be storms and thrashing windscreen wipers, fish and sharks swimming around a taxi moving apparently under water, footsteps squelching in a carpeted bank, bags of money heavy with rainwater. When the fleeing robber finally fires his pistol at the pursuing cops, the bullets fall limply from the barrel of the pistol.

One bullet gasps: "It's not the heat, it's the humidity".

And always the bank robber is sweating and disrobing, sweating and growing skinnier, weaker. Finally, he gulps a feverishly fast series of frosty beers in a pub, collapses face-down on the bar, and is handcuffed. But soon his sufferings are over. One of the cops slurps a beer and observes laconically: "It's not the heat, it's the humidity". The other cop looks down uneasily at the pub's sticky carpet, where the robber's Y-fronts, pistol, and handcuffs lie in a large puddle.

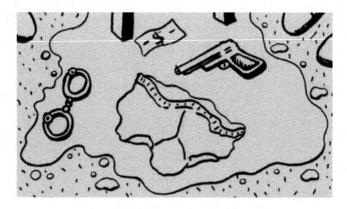

They are now the only signs that he ever existed. As the film's synopsis says: "The weather thwarts a bank robber. Then it destroys him".

*

After "Please Don't Bury Me", the next track on that John Prine vinyl record from Christchurch in 1974 is called "Christmas In Prison". It begins with a brief but sardonic and amusing observation about prison life.

> It was Christmas in prison
> And the food was really good.
> We had turkey and pistols
> Carved out of wood.[6]

However coincidental, the proximity of the two songs seems to tie together these two animated films—my first and last cartoons—more than 20 years apart. The cliché sentence repeated in *The Heat, The Humidity* is not, of course, really humorous at all. That, along with its wide currency and earnest everyday application, is part of its charm. As demonstrated by Prine in his prison song, wit is something else—or, as suggested by Max Eastman in his *The Enjoyment of Laughter*, several different things.

> Wit in its comic essence, in so far as it is distinguished from presenting ludicrous images to the imagination, consists in springing practical jokes upon the mind of the person who is expected to laugh…. An atom of humour is an unpleasantness or a frustration taken playfully…. Jokes with no point at all can be funny in an absurd way, but only if their plausibility is deftly managed, their subject matter colourful, and if surrounded with a good magnetic field of humour.[7]

As described in his autobiography *Where the Money Was*, the life of the celebrated bank robber and jail-break expert Willie Sutton (1901–1980) certainly had many of the qualities of wit. He is most famous for a witty and possibly apocryphal remark in reply to a question by Mitch Ohnstad of the *New York Herald*:

> *Ohnstad:* Why do you rob banks?
> *Sutton:* Because that's where the money is.[8]

Sutton himself always denied he ever said this. "The credit belongs to some enterprising reporter who apparently felt a need to fill out his copy. I can't even remember when I first read it. It just seemed to appear one day, and then it was everywhere."[9] In truth it is very reminiscent of Hillary's remark about why he wanted to climb Mt Everest: "Because it's there". Later, in *Chainsaw* (2007), I used the very different words—passionate, violent, romantic—of the great Spanish bullfighter Luis Miguel Dominguin on why he fought bulls: "It is like being with your lover when her husband comes in with a gun. The bull is the woman, the husband, and the pistol—all in one. No other life can give you all that".[10]

Whatever its source, and freighted with the lore of banks and money, guns and crime, Sutton's witty remark has found its way into the English language as the basis for "Sutton's Law". In medicine, this states that the most obvious diagnosis should always be considered before considering other less likely possibilities. Similar advice—the primacy of the obvious—is given in the "Willie Sutton rule" in management accounting: always look first at the areas of greatest costs to find where the greatest savings can be made.[11] But for Willie Sutton that question is the key to life itself.

> Why did I rob banks? Because I enjoyed it. I loved it. I was more alive when I was inside a bank, robbing it, than at any other time of my life. I enjoyed everything about it so much that one or two weeks later I'd be out looking for the next job.... I kept robbing banks when, by all logic, it was foolish. When it could cost me far more than I could possibly gain.[12]

This was the irrational *idée fixe* that drove Sutton. And it is, in the exaggerated way of a cartoon, what drives the bank robber in *The Heat, The Humidity*. Bergson, after Molière and Jonson, describes the *idée fixe* as the core of much comedy,[13] especially when there is a stereotypical or stock character like the cartoon masked bank robber with only one thing on his mind. Despite the obvious physical cost and his eventual demise, the robber never loses his determination to make off with the money. This is his Plan, the projected pattern of action and success that makes him smile with anticipation and excitement, like Willie Sutton, as he gazes from the plane window. And everyone the robber meets is, if not happy to be part of his plan, at least happy to talk about the weather. The repetition of: "It's not the heat, it's the humidity", with typical Queensland good humour, is part of a very different pattern that surrounds the robber—the sticky web of fate that ensnares him. His repeated difficulties with his plan, and his repeated attempts to persist with it, are the stuff of farce. And that's a tough gig: "Farce deals with the unreal, with the worst one can dream or dread. Farce is cruel, often brutal, even murderous.... Farce flouts the bounds of reason, good taste, fairness, and what we commonly think of as sanity".[14]

These two elements (farce and fate) are bound tightly together in *The Heat, The Humidity*. At the outset, the robber's treatment of the screaming boy loses any sympathy we might have had for him. From there, his trajectory is downward: in success, in comfort, and in weight. Despite his best efforts—shedding clothes and shoes, pointing his gun, and firing those limp bullets from it— there is no tragedy to this bank robber's story. Even in death he is represented by a pair of Y-fronts in a puddle.

According to Alfred Bermel, our enjoyment of such indignities in the long tradition of farce is "in part because these characters, being indestructible, are more than mortal, and also less. All characters are their creator's puppets, but the ones in farce seem especially impersonal".[15] And in cartoons, of course, as demonstrated most spectacularly with the Coyote in the "Roadrunner" shorts, the characters can die and re-appear again and again. In farce, the antagonist is often an object: a rock, a ladder, a falling tree, something delivered from the Acme company. But in *The Heat, The Humidity* the bank robber has a foe that is unseen, implacable and fatal: the weather. This is not unusual in storytelling, and is seen in very different genres. In Gordon Bok's modern American folk ballad, "Peter Kagan and the Wind", the antagonist—cruel, cold, calculating, and capable of speech—is the Wind at sea.[16] It threatens and tries to kill Kagan, the fisherman in his dory. Kagan fights his adversary, of course, but is defeated. The last words of the Wind are: "I'll freeze you". Kagan knows he can do nothing. In the end he is saved only by the love of his seal-wife, who protects him with her body.

But our bank robber has no such romantic way out. As a character in a farce his comic fate is that—if he is to achieve his goal and rob the bank—he must defy his antagonist again and again. And further, of course, that he must fail and die and become a puddle on the floor of a public bar. We laugh *at* him, not with him. His situation is so strange, and his determination so implacable, that he seems at home in a cartoon. Here he can shrink to a skinny relic, then lose all his clothes along with his dignity, and eventually all the money he has stolen at such physical cost. As a stock character in a cartoon farce, the robber in *The Heat, The Humidity* has no self-consciousness or reflective faculties, no inner life for us to see. He will never tell us, as Willie Sutton does, how it feels to rob a bank:

> During the planning of a robbery you are in a constant state of excitement. From the time you disarm the guard to the time you enter the vault, all of your juices are flowing. And then comes the exhilaration of getting into the vault, the satisfaction of the escape....[17]

Equally we know the other cartoon characters, including his "victims", only by their mostly agreeable if not sympathetic behaviour and their (repeated) observations about the weather. They too are stock characters: the airport bystanders, the cab driver, the bank teller, the barman, the thirsty cops. Even the two gasping anthropomorphic bullets deserve our empathy; given the absurd situation—and the heat and the humidity—any of us bullets would feel the same.

If there are any customers in the bank, or threats made to them by the armed robber, we don't see them. They are superfluous to the simple design and simpler problem: the absurdly slow process of the teller's squeezing water from the wads of money, and packing the wet notes into the robber's satchel. The humour is in the absurdity of the task, the time taken while he waits and sweats and his balaclava shrinks around his head, and the teller's cheerful and thoughtful demeanour as the robber struggles to remove it.

Of course, there are other possibilities for humour, even in a real bank robbery. In *Frame Analysis*, the sociologist Erving Goffman describes a 1966 robbery in San Francisco in which a "blonde teller", thinking it must be a joke, laughs at the gunman standing at her window with a .45 automatic.[18] For Goffman this is an example of "miskeying", a misreading of the "frame" of an event—in this case, that of the bank teller's amusement when the criminal is using a mortal threat to make an unauthorized withdrawal. For the comedy theorist D.H. Monro the humour in that situation, with all its danger, would be explicable in terms of several of his classes of humour, but certainly "any breach in the usual order of events".[19]

In *The Heat, The Humidity* the bank's customers too—like the teller—could console the long-suffering bank robber with that familiar phrase of patient explanation: "It's not the heat, it's the humidity". But there would be none of the grim humour that runs through "Bullet in the Brain", Tobias Wolff's brilliant five-page story about a bank robbery.[20] The irritated (and irritating) customer Anders cannot help making needless remarks to the robbers. With a pistol under his chin, he laughs at the mythological scene painted on the bank's ceiling, and then at the robber's language.

"What's so funny, bright boy?"
"Nothing."
"You think I'm comical?"
"You think I'm some kind of clown?"
"No."
"You think you can fuck with me?"
"No."
"Fuck with me again, you're history. *Capiche?*"
Anders burst out laughing. He covered his mouth with both hands and said, "I'm sorry, I'm sorry", then snorted helplessly

through his fingers and said, "*Capiche*—oh, God, *capiche*," and at that the man with the pistol raised the pistol and shot Anders right in the head.[21]

What happens next in "Bullet in the Brain" is far outside the scope of cartoon comedy or farce, and so of *The Heat, The Humidity*. But it is not, as I will show later in discussing another film, outside the range of possible subjects for animation.

With his scruples on the use of violence, the real bank robber Willie Sutton would have been disappointed and alarmed by Wolff's fictional shooting, but not surprised; he was often let down by his partners in crime. But he never hesitated to use the *threat* of violence as an essential part of his approach to robbing banks. First the pistol and later the machine gun are the tools of his trade, and in his book he is very clear about their immediate effectiveness. Yet he never mentions the psychological scars left by this clear and present mortal threat to his victims, the bank employees and customers.

Then there is the effect on the life of the non-cartoon criminal, the bank robber himself. In his book *Where the Money Is*, retired FBI Special Agent William J. Rehder addresses the romance of bank robbery in the movies: "The movies gloss over the fundamental reality of the bank robbery trade: that bank robbers' lives are either exceedingly short, or exceedingly long and boring, spent largely behind bars".[22] Having spent more than half his life behind bars—he was once sentenced by one judge to a *minimum* of 132 years[23]—Sutton can hardly deny the truth about the long years in jail. But even here he describes the excitement of a new obsession, another *idée fixe*. This time it is not the romance of robbing banks, but the determination to break out of jail. And he does not hesitate to circle back to the remark, however apocryphal, on which his fame is based, and to allude to the "enterprising reporter" who made it all possible. At the end of his life—always around criminal violence and threatening to use it but never, by his account, pulling the trigger—Sutton has his eye on a transcendent act. Or at least on beating the odds.

> Actually I spent far more time planning how to break out of jails, if only because I spent so much more time inside, trying to get out, than outside, trying to get in. If any enterprising reporter had ever asked me why I broke out of jail, I suppose that's what I would have said: 'Because I was in.' But also, you know, because there's a thrill that comes from breaking out of jail, after years of the most meticulous planning, with everybody watching you, against all the odds, that is like nothing else in the world.[24]

It should be noted that, except for the tense of one word, Rehder has taken the title of his book entirely from Sutton's *Where the Money Was*. If Willie Sutton were alive today—he died in 1980, aged 79—he would have something to say about this act of petty larceny.

And perhaps he would sympathize with the cartoon robber, who is destroyed in the tropics and lacks even a name. Trapped by his *idée fixe* and the absurd possibilities of animation, the ever-shrinking robber plays out his final hours in a dance of death with the weather itself. But as a stock character in a cartoon he can never have the excitement of Willie Sutton's criminal life—nor its price, the wasted decades in jail—or even the all-too-believable characters in Wolff's story. From cartoon ambition to extinction in less than 4 minutes, our anonymous character has only animation's "illusion of life", which is really no life at all.

*

However illusory its "life" may be, animation is not limited to the fiction and comedy of the conventional cartoon. Backed by testimony and the claim to truth, it is able to present events from the physical world with all the imaginative possibilities of the film maker. However graphic or strange or realistic its appearance, these are the feelings, experiences and visions of real people—of a

Willie Sutton—for whom life is neither illusory nor repeatable. In the animated documentary it is played—as it must be—for keeps.

NOTES

1 *Please Don't Bury Me, Dance of Death, The Darra Dogs, His Mother's Voice.*
2 Henderson, Brian. "Cartoon and Narrative" in: Horton, Andrew S. *Comedy/Cinema/Theory.* Berkeley and Los Angeles: University of California Press, 1991. 155.
3 ibid. 163.
4 Torre, Dan. *Animation – Process, Cognition and Actuality.* New York: Bloomsbury Academic, 2017. 83.
5 ibid. 83 (italics in original).
6 Prine, John. *Sweet Revenge.* Atlantic Records, 1973.
7 in Monro, D.H. *Argument of Laughter.* Carlton: Melbourne University Press, 1951. 55.
8 Sutton William and Edward Linn. *Where the Money Was: The Memoirs of a Bank Robber.* New York: Library of Larceny/Broadway Books, 2004. 135–136.
9 ibid. 135–136.
10 Anon. "Spain's greatest matador lays down his sword". Melbourne: *The Age*: 10-5-1996. 9.
11 https://en.wikipedia.org/wiki/Willie_Sutton (retrieved 19-3-20).
12 Sutton William and Edward Linn. op. cit. 134.
13 in Monro, D.H. op. cit. 40.
14 Bermel, Alfred. op. cit. 21.
15 ibid. 24.
16 Bok, Gordon. *Peter Kagan and the Wind.* Folk Legacy Records, 1971.
17 Sutton, William and Edward Linn. op. cit. 13.
18 Goffman, Erving. *Frame Analysis: An Essay on the Organization of Experience.* Boston: Northeastern University Press, 1986. 312–313.
19 Monro, D.H. op. cit. 41.
20 Wolff, Tobias. "Bullet in the Brain" in *Our Story Begins.* London: Bloomsbury, 2009. 263–268.
21 ibid. 265–266.
22 Rehder, William and Gordon Dillow. *Where the Money Is.* New York: W.W. Norton, 2003. 247–248.
23 Sutton, William and Edward Linn. op. cit. 299.
24 ibid. 135.

CHAPTER 5

Documentaries of Life and Death

AS. SOONE. AS. WEE. TO BE. BEGVNNE: WE. DID.
BEGINNE. TO. BE. VNDONE.

English memento mori *medal (c1650)[1]*

The animated documentary has a long and rich history, but the term "animated documentary" itself can at first seem an oxymoron. "Animation", after all, has usually meant "cartoons". The first book-length study of animation (Lutz, 1920) is titled *Animated Cartoons* and extends only briefly into educational animation and graphics.[2] And "documentary" has usually meant the cinematic representation of actual events, as far as possible using visible (photographic) evidence but supported by eyewitness accounts and a spoken or text narrative. There is also Grierson's famous and enduring 1933 definition of the documentary as "the creative treatment of actuality",[3] where "creative" allows for many possibilities. The confusion in terminology is symbolized in the Oscar for Best *Documentary* (not Animation) Short Subject awarded to *Neighbours* (McLaren, 1952), where the stop-motion animation of

DOI: 10.1201/9781003199663-5

live actors is used to tell a story that is clearly political but also fictional and allegorical.[4]

In responding to the sinking of the *RMS Lusitania* in 1915 by a German U-boat torpedo, with the loss of 1,200 lives, Winsor McCay had no doubt that his 1918 animated film was a *"record"* of the atrocity. One of the early inter-title cards says: "From here on you are looking at the first record of the sinking of the Lusitania". It was of course the only visual "record" possible when there were no cameras to document the event itself. McCay creates a powerfully visual account in a remarkably realistic style, a tribute to his virtuosic drawing and his sense of directorial timing, scale, and drama. But there are also signs of his earlier illustrative work: the cartoon fish in the underwater scenes, the massed anonymity of the human figures, the stylized "nouveau smoke" from the ship's funnels with its violent movement and sense of the macabre.[5] The weight of individual lives lost is borne not by character animation but by photographs of some of the more famous dead. In addition to its clear purpose as wartime propaganda, *The Sinking of the Lusitania* is even today a remarkably moving film, not only for the tragedy it presents with such empathy and accuracy but also for McCay's determination and preternatural skills.

The absence of actual footage remains an important justification for the animated documentary. In fact, absence is a recurring theme in Honess Roe's *Animated Documentary*, first in discussing the ontology of the genre: "Animation *substitutes* or it *evokes*. Both terms imply an absence—an absence of original filmed material due to practical constraints or impossibilities".[6] And later, more specifically in relation to memory and certain filmmakers: "The absence of indexical images speaks to the absences in knowledge and memory that several of these filmmakers have in relation to their pasts. The process of making the films is, in a way, a performative act of becoming that which reconnects them with history".[7]

The possible reasons for these absences have multiplied since *The Sinking of the Lusitania*—though in its various manifestations death remains both a prominent and permanent one—as have the means by which animation can act as a document. Not only can dinosaurs walk the earth again via CGI, but human experience can be represented visually in many different ways. Even in the age of the mobile phone camera, wearable cameras and live streaming, few lives are documented cinematically or photographically in any but the most fleeting moments. For the rest of life's physical reality and the immense range of human emotional experience we still rely on verbal accounts in voice or text and on visual re-creations, animated or otherwise.

Unlike the live action documentary, which can use many creative cinematic techniques to mould its claimed representation of photographic reality, animation is separate from the documentary subject it examines. Historical or predictive, it may be based on research or memory or both, but importantly it does not influence the subject. As Ülo Pikkov says:

> Therefore, it can be argued—at least theoretically—that in a sense animations depict their subjects even more objectively than conventional documentaries, because they recreate the essence of the subject through an application of an appropriate animation technique without actually filming, and thus influencing, it.[8]

This possible influence on the subject, and animation's freedom from its contagion, may be true of observational documentaries that have no written and narrated script. It is much less applicable to the documentary made with a familiar formula: archival footage or stills (more or less relevant and in context), interviews, graphics, and new footage of a physical setting, all held together with illustrative sound and music, and a highly interpretative and often manipulative voice-over and/or presenter. It could be argued ("at least theoretically") that such conventional live action documentaries are, in their veiled confidence, even more subjective than many animated documentaries, which are usually at pains to prove their specific claim to truth, in the face of the inevitable doubt manifest in every animated frame.

NOTES

1 Enright, D.J. (ed) *The Oxford Book of Death*. Oxford, New York. Oxford University Press. 1983. 4.

2 Lutz, E.G. op. cit.

3 Quoted in: Honess Roe, Annabelle. *Animated Documentary*. London, New York: Palgrave Macmillan, 2013. 3.

4 https://en.wikipedia.org/wiki/Neighbours_(1952_film) retrieved 10-10-20.

5 Bukatman, Scott. *The Poetics of Slumberland*. Berkeley: University of California Press, 2012. 95.

6 Honess Roe, Annabelle. *Animated Documentary*. 27 (italics in original).

7 ibid. 168.

8 Pikkov, Ulo. *Animasophy: Theoretical Writings on the Animated Film*. Tallinn: Estonian Academy of Arts, 2010. 96.

CHAPTER 6

The Darra Dogs (1993)

Can I have a dog?

ZELDA TUPICOFF, AGED 5 (1990)

As a rite of parenthood this question from our young daughter was to be expected, but it was difficult to answer. As adults we saw the practical issues: our small yard, the responsibilities of looking after a pet, the question of breeds, and other complications and difficulties. But there were some other concerns for me: episodes with powerful images and intense feelings that I remembered from my childhood. A few nights later, talking to some friends, I tried to explain just what these were. As the stories came out, my voice wavered, my heart raced, my body shook. Someone suggested these experiences, or my memories of them, would make an interesting film.

By now I had made many animated TV commercials, in whole or in part, and several commissioned shorts, usually on health issues like smoking and dental care. *Dance of Death* had won awards at international festivals and had screened theatrically around Australia with a Mel Brooks feature. I was also no stranger to film "reality" in the form of live action, nor to writing fictional scripts; I had written and directed *The Bear* (1989), a 30 minute short, mainly live action, about an animator suddenly

DOI: 10.1201/9781003199663-6

taken over by one of his cartoon characters. I had also directed a short special effects test sequence with glowing skeletons for one of the planned live action features. But *The Darra Dogs*, steeped as it was in memory, was always going to be animated.

When I sat down to write my memories as storyboards and drawings and scribbles, they poured out in less than 2 days.

28

One lunchtime we heard the crack of a rifle, and the yelp of a dog.

I ran to the corner opposite the House of Lights,

The dog ran limping past, followed by a Roman Catholic priest with a rifle.

At this speed, the process was one of transcription or recording rather than writing in any more imaginative sense. Several of the action sequences were already in shot order, with screen direction, point of view and composition already clear; others appeared as just one image. Some were more distinct than others, but all were filled in with memories of my thoughts as a child. These would be the basis for the voice-over script, a much longer process.

Now I faced a jumble of discrete sequences and images—and remembered sounds—that had no shape as a film. How should I tell this fractured story? What should be first or last? There were no independent chronological records, no archives or dated images, and certainly no home movies. In fact there were very few photographic images of my childhood at all, and only two images of all our family's Darra dogs.

In a live action film, the director has many choices to make within physical, stylistic, and budget limitations. To these can be added, in animation, more fundamental decisions about the image itself: not only lighting and composition and visual "feel", but the very form of the image, and how it is to be produced, what will be added to an entirely blank screen. The director in animation—as an auteur, a kind of God in the film's universe—does not frame the image or even interpret it, but *creates* it. In this film I wanted each sequence to have its own look, within my limited graphic range. This decision was made easier by my determination to keep to my child's eye point of view. While retaining my eye-witness claim to truth, and using my voice as adult narrator, I never appear in the film. In fact except for shadows only one human figure ever appears: the priest who shoots the dog and then bashes it to death.

And the dogs—whether monsters or playful pups or helpless victims, in blue or yellow or black—are never anthropomorphic. They certainly never speak or stand on two legs. In discussing the Disney cartoons, Richard Schickel describes the adaptation of "adult" silent comedy routines for a general audience, taking the movement and timing but losing the often objectionable tone: "What had been nasty as a form of human behaviour became acceptably adorable as obviously fictive animal behaviour".[1] Scratching, licking, barking, or running, these Darra dogs are always dogs.

The film's storyboard, though drawn roughly in black texta, is a very detailed visual plan. The design is also made clear in "A Note on Design" that is bound with the storyboard.

> The graphic design of this film will reflect the different textures of these events in my memory. Though using mainly cel-and-drawing techniques, it will not be a 'cartoon' in its representation of dogs and the world. By using different styles, I hope to achieve the expressive truth of each sequence. These are some of the visual styles to be used:
>
> Priest and Dog: Almost completely black and completely white, rather like a lino-cut. Very broadly drawn, with only occasional highlights of colour eg: the lights of the house, the blood, etc.
>
> Dog in Creek: Extremely detailed, in both full view and details, so that the audience can study the scene, as I did. The large artwork will be based on photographs, with lots of tiny detailed movement (ripples, hair, water insects) as well as a spider and a butterfly or two.
>
> Pack of Dogs: Burnt-out images: predominantly white, with colour mainly in the shadows.[2]

These notes are followed closely in the film. They describe a drawn image but do not address the question of how the images are to be drawn or—more precisely—*arrived at.* Unlike the cinematographer, who is tied to the photographic and a series of "decisive moments" of filmed reality, the animator-as-God has many tools from charcoal to brush to (today) 2D and 3D computer animation, to motion capture and its traditional cousin, the rotoscope. "Rotoscoping" has taken various forms over the last century, but essentially it is the use of live action moving-image material (existing or shot for purpose) as an aid to achieving more or less "lifelike" animated movement. But in creating believable characters with human emotions but animal movement, as Disney discovered, the animator's imagination was needed. Reference material was shot on film for *101 Dalmatians* (Geronimi et al., 1961), "but the scenes that brought characters to life were the ones imagined by the animator, showing what the dog could have done, in ways the dog would have done it".[3]

From my own television commercials and seeing other films I was aware of rotoscope's ability to produce drawings of realistic movement, but it never seemed appropriate for this film. It was true that "the dead dogs of my childhood were still alive within me", but they were not as they once were. They were memories and I, whose mind had retained those memories—with the often-disturbing emotions associated with them—was no longer a child. As someone self-trained in cartoon animation, however, I had never animated a four-legged animal. So my decision to draw the film from memory, without rotoscoping, led to a lengthy study of dog anatomy (especially the skeleton), the photographic sequences of Edweard Muybridge, and various films, both animated and live action. I also did many sketches from memory. Fortunately these memories were plentiful, and became the basis of the film in fact as well as in ambition.

Ironically, despite all this work, *The Darra Dogs* has often been seen (and sometimes "suspected") as an example of rotoscoping.

In post-production, every film is constructed from available materials and shaped into its final form: the only form an audience will see. For many documentaries, a vast amount of visual material (archival and new footage, interviews and graphics) can be assembled and then cut down to a manageable size. But an *animated* documentary is unlikely to have very much footage to cut. Animation is usually very tedious and expensive to produce; the whole process of developing the storyboard into a film aims, at least for me, at using *everything*. But not necessarily in the original order—especially when, in its primary function of presenting experience in a powerful and truthful way, the animation fails.

As scripted and storyboarded, the final action scene in *The Darra Dogs* was to be an experience of threat and mystery, rather than actual violence. Centred on the cone of a street light on a dusty suburban road at night, the script tries to describe the mounting threat of a large and savage dog, audibly approaching but not yet visible in the darkness beyond the light. The original storyboard has this narration over five pages and 20 picture panels:

> Suddenly every sound in me and around me came from the dog. I already felt the dog's hot breath on my neck, the bony claws and the convulsions of teeth, hair and blood as it tore me open. As the invisible monster hurtled through the darkness towards me, I stood there staring at the blue cone of light, with the dust slowly swirling in it. The dog's presence filled me: Death was an immanent force in the world. Then it appeared: a huge Alsatian, running in slow motion. At first it had no shadow. It was like a two-dimensional mask, a picture of the Beast. The Wolf was coming to eat me up, dragging its shadow behind it. The shadow shortened as the dog ran beneath the light. I could no longer see its face—just the light running along its bristling back and tail. Now the black shadow of Death began racing towards me, faster than the dog itself, as I floated in mid-air.

At this point my memory fades to white. I can't remember what else happened that night. It is my strongest image of fatal terror, of Death incarnate: the empty light filled with sound and fury, the dog and its shadow, the loss of memory just as the shadow reaches out to me.

I cut all this voice-over to: "The shadow of Death raced towards me. I remember nothing else." The scene was also shortened, and moved from its climactic position in the storyboard to a less prominent and demanding place earlier in the film. The truth was that, despite my best efforts, the scene failed to deliver its promised impact. In my memory it was—and is, as the original wordy narration testified—"my strongest image of fatal terror, of Death incarnate". But as cinema, despite my best efforts in direction, design and animation, it just wasn't. The memory of that terror, far beyond the cliché "hair-raising", remained unexpressed and uncommunicated.

Many live action documentaries have little or no narration or voice-over. The work of Frederick Wiseman, for example, is generally observational and uses solely "live" voices as part of the film's edited narrative.[4] Most live action documentaries provide visual evidence, in stills or moving images, as well as interviews and other voices to support that narrative.

Some animated films document apparently lived experience in powerfully graphic form and make observations of reality without narration.[5] But most animated documentaries rely on the voice as witness or based on research—either narrated or on-screen as animated lip-sync—to make the film's claim to being a documentary. Usually the voice provides the "audible evidence"—as true as "visual evidence", but as testimony—of an event, as context and narration to accompany the animation. The narration script, if there is one, can be cut or re-written and re-recorded during the editing process. This was done twice in *The Darra Dogs* on the last day of editing. In both cases true statements in my narration were cut to keep the focus on the dogs and my observations of them, rather than on my beliefs and experiences.

The first was at the end of the sequence in which I see a priest shoot a dog and then bash it to death. As written and recorded, my original narration said: "Since that day I've never liked or trusted priests or churches". This was and is true. I could have said more: that I still recall this act of savage cruelty whenever religion is mentioned. Whatever thoughts or experiences of religion may have preceded or followed it, this eye-witness childhood memory stands as a permanent break with religious belief itself. But the scene is powerful enough to imply something like this, in an understated way, and without the grandiloquence.

The second last-minute cut to the original scripted storyboard (1990) was even more personal. At the beginning of *The Darra Dogs* storyboard, immediately after the title, there was a photograph of my two brothers and I, the only existing studio portrait of the three of us as children.

The voice-over narration says: "This is me, the youngest of three boys. This is my brother Gary, and this is Ross. It was Ross who really loved dogs." In a photograph of our backyard, a smiling Ross sits on the grass with a small black dog: "He had dogs his whole life". And at the end of the storyboard we return to the studio portrait, zooming in on the middle brother in the group of three, Ross: "After he left home, my brother Ross had many dogs. He raced, bred, and showed them successfully. He even designed and built a dog-exercising machine, using an old washing-machine motor. He died in 1973, after a motor-bike accident. He was 26, with a wife and a 2-year-old son". The narration continues as the sequence (and the storyboard) ends with a zoom into my face in the same group portrait. I am about 4 years old: "I am now 39, and I live in Melbourne. I haven't had a pet since we lived in Darra. But our daughter is 5 years old, and she wants to have a dog. I don't know what to say to her".

In test screenings there was a strong feeling that the audience was unprepared for this late return to my dead brother, that it distracted from the main subject of the film—it was always titled *The Darra Dogs*—and that it gave insufficient time to reflect on Ross and his place in the narrative. The consensus was that, in such a short film, it was an unnecessary complication that compromised both my brother's story and that of the dogs he loved. My acceptance of this view also brought into question the use of the photograph of Ross sitting on the grass with one of the dogs, and indeed the place of photographs in the film. There were only two photographic images of dogs anyway; perhaps I should concentrate on the dogs as animated memories and leave out the photographic brothers entirely. Suddenly these two forms of memory—the teeming mass of drawn memories and the few photographs of reality, the quick and the dead—stood in opposition to each other. As director, producer and editor I had to choose.

In its final form, cut on the last day of editing from 12 to 10 minutes, the film has no photographs. And the emotional climax is not "the Wolf was coming to eat me up" under the street light, as written and storyboarded. It is the priest's murder of the dog, followed by my meditation, as a child, on the rotting body of a dog in a creek. The film ends with a gaudy sunset and my voice: "I haven't had a pet since we left Darra nearly 30 years ago. Now our young daughter wants to have a dog. But the dead dogs of my childhood are still alive within me. I don't know what to say to her".

Any documentary makes a claim to truth. Even a mockumentary depends for its humour on its awareness of truth in style, performance and content, and where and how the boundaries can be drawn, stretched, and violated. *The Darra Dogs* sets out to present some memories of a childhood (mine) that was almost completely undocumented in images or in writing. In doing so, with my voice-over representing me as the key witness, it asks that drawn scenes of animated movement—visual evidence that is non-photographic—be accepted as true.

Elsewhere I will discuss the work of various writers on photography and cinema. For now, with memory and animation in mind, I want to mention Barthes' observation that in the cinema "photography's *having-been-there* gives way before a *being-there* of the thing... a more projective, more 'magical' fictional consciousness".[6] Writing in 1927, Kracauer compares memory to photography:

> An individual retains memories because they are personally significant.... Since what is significant is not reducible to either merely spatial or merely temporal terms, memory images are at odds with photographic representation.[7]

Further, Kracauer goes on to claim that "the meaning of memory images is linked to their truth content.... All memory images... may rightly be called the last image, since it alone preserves the unforgettable".[8] In Barthes' terms, animated memories might be termed "remembering-being-there", with memory embodied "truthfully" in the animated image, in a way impossible with photography. In *The Darra Dogs*, drawn from memory with all its flaws but with its own truth, the photograph has no place. But this animated truth—like so many others in life—is complicated, and not always *exactly* true from every point of view. Its central claim is that of accurate memory—a claim that, if tested on the facts of visible evidence, the film sometimes clearly fails.

First there are the obvious liberties taken with graphic expression. Did I ever *really* see anything in pure black and pure white? Then there are the aerial shots—our front yard with a dead dog lying on the grass, the whole suburb in an establishing shot, zooming in—that, without access to a helicopter or large balloon, I clearly never saw. There is also the shot that tracks beside a collie dog as it runs in slow motion, its ears back and its long golden hair streaming, as the bush background glides past in an idealized scene of canine motion.

Early in the dog/priest sequence I maintain my point of view from behind the school fence at lunchtime. But this is soon dispensed with. When the priest has shot the dog, and closes in for the kill, we see the dog's terrified face from the priest's point of view, intercut with shots of his advancing feet. Soon we see the raised rifle butt from the dog's abject point of view, and hold the shot as the rifle plunges down towards him and us, cutting to black on impact.

If these are sins of commission, there are also sins of omission. With judicious framing the audience is, for instance, denied (or spared) the full visual details of the dog's killing, which in fact I saw and remember clearly.

While the piece of wood rises and falls relentlessly in the hand of the priest—in craft terms, an economical animated cycle—the bottom of frame is a curtain drawn across the bashed dog. (The sound, however—a cabbage hacked in the sound studio—spares us nothing.) Equally the film does not show the blood and brains on the grassy footpath that I passed on my way home that afternoon. And I don't mention my cousin Wayne, who was there at the fence with me and remembers the event too, as a corroborating witness.

Le Sang des bêtes/Blood of the Beasts (Franju, 1949) has a very different approach to animals and violence. Shot in Paris, four of its nine sequences show, in all its bloody reality and cruelty, the slaughter of animals for meat. Its point, as Jeannette Sloniowski says, is "that death is real, that it is both gruesome and violent but also that it can be aesthetically beautiful at the same time".[9] Like *The Darra Dogs,* this live action film refuses to anthropomorphize the animals whose suffering and deaths it documents. But *The Darra Dogs* is set in memory—another country—and it forsakes the brutal reality of life for my animated visions of a long-ago childhood: a varied but particular "illusion of life". *Blood of the Beasts,* on the other hand, refuses to use any of the strategies that might distance the viewer from the visible evidence of an urban slaughterhouse. We are spared nothing: "The cruelty in the film is cold and unmelodramatic. No emotional energy is wasted in the pursuit of pathos or romance. One butcher sips a cup of something while skinning an animal; another sings 'La Mer' while hosing down the blood-drenched floors".[10]

Several scenes in *The Darra Dogs* are announced or inferred as memories but are, on the evidence, childhood fantasies: the dog's sickening unto death in the shimmering moonlight while I sleep, before we find its stiff body on the grass in the morning; the abusive home of the dog-nappers who, I try to believe, have stolen our dog; and my vain hopes for a happy return of the "stolen" dog. As such they are "real" memories; but how real can a memory be after at least 30 years, and with all the evidence of animated invention confessing its non-reality throughout?

None of these observations is meant to deny the essential emotional truth of the events I present in *The Darra Dogs*, or my memory of them. But there is always a distance between the ordinariness of everyday life—and violence, and death—as it passes by, and its translation by the language of cinema into another form of reality. Animation is yet another language (or languages) with many more dialects and accents, that goes back much further than *The Jazz Singer* or the Lumiere brothers or Niépce, to the first shadows on a wall, the first stories, the first marks on the ground.

*

Before embarking on *The Darra Dogs*, I visited Darra with my brother Gary and a video camera. With Gary driving the car, I shot various places of significance in the film: our old house, the "house of lights" where the priest shot the dog (now with aluminium sliding-glass replacing its "cheap coloured-glass windows"), the ragged skylines of gum trees, and many other details for reference in the film's design. Some of the shots had dogs visible here and there, but they were incidental. I had no interest in more study of dog movement or anatomy. It was a quiet afternoon in this working-class suburb of Brisbane.

Though I was interested only in the images, and only for rough reference, I had left the camcorder's microphone switched on. Only much later, when reviewing the footage, did I notice the soundtrack was full of dogs. There were other sounds, of course, in this accidental "wild atmos" recording of a suburb on a weekday afternoon: the low hum of cars on the highway nearby, individual cars as they came and went, voices of unseen people, and birds, and various occasional mechanical sounds. Gary and I spoke occasionally. But whether the dogs were visible or not, their sound was always there: near and far, and infinitely varied in pitch, tone, and purpose. Recorded accidentally, these were the descendants of the dogs of my childhood, still alive in Darra, still going about their canine business mostly unseen, and now part of my archive.

NOTES

1 Quoted in: Wells, Paul. *Animation: Genre and Authorship*. London: Wallflower, 2002. 56.
2 Tupicoff, Dennis. Storyboard for *the Darra Dogs*. (unpublished, 1990).
3 Thomas, Frank and Ollie Johnston. *Disney Animation: The Illusion of Life*. New York: Abbeville Press, 1981. 343.
4 Wiseman, Frederick. *Titicut Follies* (1967), *National Gallery* (2014) etc.
5 Cournoyer, Michèle. *The Hat* (1999); Hodgson, Jonathan. *Night Club* (1983).
6 quoted in: Doane, Mary Ann. *The Emergence of Cinematic Time*. Cambridge, MA.: Harvard University Press, 2002. 103.
7 Kracauer, Siegfried. *The Mass Ornament: Weimar Essays*. Cambridge, MA: Harvard University Press, 1995. 50
8 ibid. 51.
9 Sloniowski, Jeannette in: Grant, Barry Keith and Jeannette Sloniowski (eds). *Documenting the Documentary*. Detroit: Wayne State University Press, 1998. 186.
10 ibid. 186.

CHAPTER 7

His Mother's Voice (1997)

And I was swinging from hope to death, to hope, to death. And thinking all the time: I need to keep it together. I need to keep it together.

KATHY EASDALE. ABC RADIO INTERVIEW:
THE WORLD TODAY (1995)

One lunchtime in May 1995 I was listening to the ABC's *The World Today* on our old kitchen radio. The story was about the recent shooting death of a teenager named Matthew Easdale in my home town of Brisbane. After one or two preliminary questions and brief answers, the interviewer (Matt Brown) asked Matthew's mother:

Q: How did you first learn about Matthew's death?

Kathy Easdale's answer was an uninterrupted 6′30″ narrative monologue that began by setting the time and place of the initial phone call from a neighbour.

DOI: 10.1201/9781003199663-7

> A: Oh, I'd gone to bed, and the phone rang… just… I guess it was not long after midnight. And it was Mrs Booth… and she was like… screaming. And she said: Kathy, Matthew's been shot. Please come quickly.

Kathy then described each of the unfolding events very clearly and sequentially, until the story's tragic denouement and its aftermath. Yet I was soon in tears. A friend had to pull over while listening to the same broadcast; she could no longer see to drive her car. Such a long monologue by an interviewee is almost unknown in broadcast journalism; it had clearly left its mark on the people at ABC radio. As Kathy spoke I had seen a whole series of dramatic images and from her point of view as the storyteller. There were midnight faces and houses and cars and doorways: a dark and dramatic nightmare of hope and despair, of waiting for good news when everything looked bad. Immediately I knew that I wanted to see these images on screen, to bring them to life with Kathy's voice as an animated film. But that voice was so powerful on its own. Why illustrate it? What could I possibly add to Kathy's extraordinary account?

Several months later—I think it was on a plane somewhere—I suddenly had the idea of showing another point of view, another version of the same interview. There are of course as many mental versions of a radio interview as there are listeners. But the interview had been recorded somewhere. That was enough for me.

Responsibility—to the subject, to history, to reality, to truth—lies at the heart of any documentary, animated or not. In an autobiographical film like *The Darra Dogs* the storyteller's responsibility is largely to one's self—and the truth of one's memories. But in biography or current affairs there is a responsibility to those whose story one is telling. If trauma is involved, this responsibility can weigh heavily. With all its evidence of very personal trauma, I wanted Kathy's permission to use the original recording. As a film maker I also needed it; the ABC, as the broadcaster which owned the recording, made this a condition of its use in the film. Kathy and I corresponded, and we talked on the phone. I explained that I had no interest in the controversial aspects of the case, which was national news, or with the political dimension of the gun ownership debate. Nor would I need to interview her, or even meet for background research; I was interested only in her voice and the story she told in the radio interview. We made an arrangement to meet when I visited Brisbane from Melbourne, but the meeting was postponed and eventually never took place. With Kathy's written permission, though, the 1/4" audio tape was delivered to me by the ABC.

During this time the details of the production fell rapidly into place. Without any evidence except the interview itself, I decided that it was recorded in Kathy's living room. This was also Matthew's home, with his things everywhere—but without Matthew. By now I had listened to Kathy's story many times; it had become precious and inviolable. Despite all the dramatic ellipses of her narrative, reflected in the cinematic cuts in Part 1 from one location to another, from one neighbour or teenager or police officer to another, I knew that the interview had been recorded in real time. So for Part 2 could it also be shown, cinematically, in real time? Six minutes and 30 seconds was a long time for a talking head but not for a single-shot journey around the house and yard, a real-time trip through Matthew's world while Kathy spoke into the microphone. Now the film was a diptych, a pair of films with the same voice driving each of them: one set in the past and dramatic, loud and strong; the other "live" in the present, calm and quiet, in the time and place of recording.

Only years later did I realize that I was looking not only for a more imaginative way to interpret or illustrate the interview, but also for a way to see—and feel—the source of the interview's power, which beat out so strongly in every syllable of Kathy's voice. Having two versions—two points of view—made it possible to see a (metaphorically) stereo view of the event, both then and now: the past, where hope (or its memory) survived, and the present, where everything was known. Almost incidentally I now had a simple but expressive title (*His Mother's Voice*) that also recalled the old painting of a dog and a phonograph that became the famous logo for "His Master's Voice" (HMV).[1] I prepared a detailed storyboard and applied successfully for federal funding.

and when I got there one of the boys
that was with Matthew had run back

and I asked him,
the first thing I asked him was,

is Matthew OK?
And he said yes

In keeping with the "serial/stereo" approach to the film's narrative, each of the two parts of the film was traced and drawn by a different hand. I drew Part 1 directly onto cels with the thick black lines and shadows from *The Darra Dogs*; Annette Trevitt adapted her own charcoal drawing technique for Part 2. Like the mix of live action and animation in the form of rotoscope, the production process was a hybrid: digital from shoot to edit and the thousands of A4 frame prints for rotoscoping; an old-style use of paper and charcoal, cels and paint, with a rostrum shoot and the cut on 35 mm. It was to be my last use of non-digital production techniques.

Kathy's voice was necessarily the centrepiece throughout. Her monologue was always to remain uncut—though some viewers would later claim that one half or the other was longer—and at the centre of the sound design. In Part 1 all the shots, design and action had to fit into the rhythms and words of Kathy's story. In Part 2 both actors had to learn their on-screen lines as both text and performance, with all the breaths and pauses and lip sounds in place, so their lip sync would be accurate and easy to rotoscope with the accuracy required. Their performances are controlled—*animated*—by the voice of Kathy Easdale, just as the rest of the film is controlled by me as director.

As Michel Chion says: "The idea of dubbing was born with the sound film itself".[2] Beginning with its critical use in Hitchcock's first talkie *Blackmail* (1929), Chion goes on to describe the sequence in *Singin' in the Rain* (Kelly/Donen, 1952) in which a rising curtain reveals Debbie Reynolds to be Jean Hagen's singing voice: "An astonishing shot reveals the two women, one behind the other, with the two microphones lined up, both singing with this single voice that wanders between them looking for its source".[3] In *His Mother's Voice* one woman's voice also passes for another, though in a very different way. The audience already knows that this is a *radio* interview and that, despite the "acoustical indexicality"[4] of Kathy Easdale's recorded voice, the images are obviously animated without any claim to the recorded reality of the photographic or the live action cinematic image. And all the animation is drawn via rotoscope from the bodies and faces of actors, as listed in the film's credits. But there is much more to Kathy Easdale's voice, and its importance to the film, than this.

By the time we see the drawings of Leverne McDonnell playing the role of "Kathy Easdale" in Part 2, Kathy's voice has become firmly established in Part 1 as the visually absent *acousmêtre* defined by Chion: "a special being, a kind of talking and acting shadow... the one who is not-yet-seen, but who remains liable to appear in the visual field at any moment".[5] Earlier he takes us back to the womb: "The fetus takes in the mother's voice, and will recognize it after birth.... In the infant's experience, the mother ceaselessly plays hide-and-seek with his visual field, whether she goes behind him, or is hidden from him by something, or if he's right up against her body and cannot see her".[6]

The words of many other people are reported by Kathy in Part 1 of *His Mother's Voice*, but always with her voice as acousmêtre. Beginning her account with a close-up of a blood red phone and its rhythmically swinging cord, Kathy says that the phone rang.

"And it was Mrs Booth on the other end, and she was like... screaming. And she was saying: Kathy, Matthew's been shot. Please come quickly". Chion maintains that the telephone and the gramophone (and, I would argue, the radio) have, in separating voices from bodies, come to remind us of the dead.[7] He cites Proust's description of his grandmother's acousmatic voice on the telephone: "A real presence, perhaps, that voice that seemed so near—in actual separation! But a premonition also of an eternal separation! Many were the times, as I listened thus without seeing her who spoke to me, that the voice was crying to me from the depths out of which one does not rise again…".[8]

The beloved's lips and the telephone have always had a close association. In the slow country song, the intimate voice of Jim Reeves saves the drama and high stakes for the last line:

> Put your sweet lips a little closer to the phone.
> Let's pretend that we're together, all alone.
> I'll tell the man to turn the jukebox way down low
> And you can tell your friend there with you
> He'll have to go.[9]

But as acousmêtre we see neither Kathy's lips nor her face; at first only a black shadow moves across the phone and the swinging cord. Soon we will see only her wide unblinking eyes in the rear view mirror, the lights of passing cars dazzling her as she drives to the house where Matthew has been shot.

The rest of Kathy's face, and particularly her mouth, is hidden from us, even as her voice bears the weight of the narrative. The de-acousmatization of her voice, "the unveiling of an image and at the same time a *place*, the human and mortal body where the voice will henceforth be lodged",[10] takes place only at the beginning of Part 2. Drawn in shimmering charcoal, the microphone materializes out of darkness and moves towards the sitting figure of Christopher Connelly (playing the journalist Matt Brown) as he mimes with Brown's original taped voice: "How did you first learn about Matthew's death?" The camera's point of view moves with the microphone to reveal Leverne McDonnell as Kathy, also seated in mid-shot.

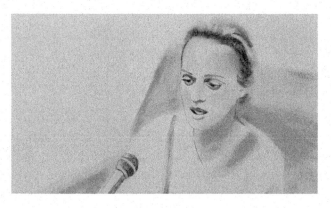

As the point of view moves in towards her face, she begins her now-familiar story exactly as before: "Oh, I'd gone to bed, and the phone rang...". From now on, despite her animated form, Kathy is both mortal and vulnerable. Having secured her to a place in the room, the point of view moves on through the house, and then the world outside, for the next 5 minutes.

The whole of Part 2 was conceived and storyboarded as one continuous shot. For various reasons, however—performance, cueing a car (and later a dog) to pass through the frame at the right moment, variations in timing—there were not one but many live action shots for Part 2. These would have been impossible to join seamlessly in live action. But the sketchy style of animation used in Part 2 made it possible to draw the necessary "in-betweens" to join each shot to the next, to achieve the "single" shot required.

When it finally returns to the house, near the end of Part 2, the same drifting point of view moves across Kathy's living room towards her. Now she repeats the fatal words of the ambulance man we heard in Part 1 (which was then set behind a darkened ambulance with the shock of one photographer's flash): "Your son Matthew's been shot and we're sorry...". Now the drawn charcoal lips of Leverne McDonnell fill the screen with their precise lip sync, like Kane's dying word "Rosebud" in *Citizen Kane* (Welles, 1941): "...but he's passed away". From this moment of finality the point of view moves up to her eyes, then into one eye, then into the shimmering darkness of the eye itself.

In an interview for Judith Kriger's book *Animated Realism* I try to explain why Kathy's monologue *as audio* is "something extraordinary":

> (She has) a remarkable sense of storytelling. It's probably innate. My theory is that Kathy Easdale is a natural-born storyteller. This interview was given about ten days after (the shooting) had actually happened, so she had probably told the story many times, to police and others, so she had probably rehearsed it by virtue of telling it many times to different people.[11]

In a factual sense her narrative is extremely lean and clear. Starting with the time and place of the phone call from Mrs Booth, Kathy's account moves in chronological order to several places and many people. The ambulance man delivers the climactic moment in words, but in Kathy's voice; the grief of Matthew's brother is a coda described by Kathy, their mother. There are very few adjectives in her account, even when she is describing extremely traumatic emotions: "I felt my heart and my body disconnected". But Kathy's voice is more than a vehicle for description.

> In addition, there's an extremely strong rhythm in her voice, which I only discovered when I was "reading" the soundtrack of her voice for lip sync purposes. To me,

these things explained why it is so powerful. It has altered my view about what makes sound powerful. We all speak in a kind of rhythm. In her monologue that you hear in the film, she speaks for six and a half minutes without a break in that rhythm. In fact, you can tap it out on your knee, and you'll see that it's 26 frames per beat, without a break—until fairly close to the end, when she starts getting more upset, and then it goes up to 28. What is song but words in rhythm? She's actually "singing" a song of love and grief to her deceased son.... (T)he interviewer lets her go on, and she strikes this rhythm and she's told it before, and it's therefore exactly like a song.[12]

In trying to identify the power of Kathy's voice, a term from Roland Barthes comes to mind. In his essay *The Grain of Voice*, Barthes discusses *"the encounter between a language and a voice"*, using the examples of two (for him) very different singers: Panzera and Fischer-Diskau.[13] There is perhaps in Kathy Easdale's "song" the *geno-song* as described by Barthes: "That apex... where the melody really works at the language—not at what it says, but... where the melody explores how the language works and identifies with that work.... The song must speak, must *write*—for what is produced at the level of the genotype is finally writing".[14]

In his script for *The Night of the Hunter* (Laughton, 1955), James Agee is careful to include the singing voice of the old woman (Lillian Gish) to balance that of the psychopath (Robert Mitchum), and to save the two children. As Marguerite Duras says in her moving account: "The song becomes the wall that crime cannot scale during the passing of the night".[15] Sadly for Kathy Easdale, her song of love and loss cannot be that wall to protect Matthew; it seems that he died almost instantly. *In memoriam*, Kathy's voice will always be too late.

As an animated documentary, *His Mother's Voice* is probably best known for the fact that it presents two narrative versions of the same ABC radio interview. In constructing those visual narratives, however, the film's two re-enactments borrow heavily from the narrative tradition of the fiction film. The two parts of the film are as different as possible, within the constraints of the rotoscope technique and its direct connection to the image of live action re-enactment. Both elements of the film—the doubling of the interview and the many deliberate differences between the two parts—have been widely described and appreciated. But another aspect is rarely mentioned: the use of a *different* subjective point of view in each part. With Kathy Easdale's wringing hands, mirror reflection, and blurred images, Part 1 is clearly from her own point of view. Part 2, with Kathy revealed as a talking interview subject sitting in her living room, is just as clearly from another point of view. The source or character behind this point of view is never identified and will be left open to interpretation here. But it is important to investigate what happens on screen in each part of *His Mother's Voice*, and why.

Radio, like anything in the acoustic world, has no visual frame. Animation, on the other hand, replaces or fills up a cinema frame which would otherwise be empty, since in radio there is no live action as either a source or illustration of the voice. To make them work together, to show something meaningful while Kathy is speaking, it is necessary to construct an animated visual world that makes sense of both the audio *and* the animated images. And to do it twice.

The true point of view shot (or *first-person*, or *subjective* camera shot) is almost as old as the cinema itself. From the first time a camera was fixed to the front of a moving train, in 1897, the audience was able to feel the sense of moving into and through a real landscape: "The term *phantom ride* was applied because the position of the camera meant that only the track and scenery could be seen and the movement appeared to be coming from an invisible force".[16] In later narrative cinema this "invisible force", often seen through a character's eyes, becomes a question of identity. Whose point of view are we seeing? Who is in control, cinematically? Who is in control of the narrative? Many directors have used the subjective camera briefly to make the viewer "uneasy" if the camera "actually occupies the place of the character in that position", as discussed by Jean-Pierre Oudart.[17] As "the master of suspense", Hitchcock often deploys this method in such films as *Strangers on a Train* (1951) with Miriam's murder, and *Rear Window* (1954). The question can be more specific than identity: *why* are we not seeing the character? In *Dark Passage* (Delbert Daves, 1947), for instance, the subjective point of view is used in the early scenes so that the face of the protagonist (Humphrey Bogart) can be hidden. Only after his plastic surgery is his "new" face revealed. *Lady in the Lake* (Robert Montgomery, 1947), an adaptation of Raymond Chandler's first-person novel, is shot almost entirely with a subjective point of view. The film does, however, make use of mirrors to reveal the protagonist (Montgomery himself) several times.

The view "through the character's eyes" has sometimes been taken very literally. In *A Matter of Life and Death* there are several shots from David Niven's subjective point of view in hospital as his character "Peter Carter" is wheeled into surgery, and then prepared for his brain operation. (There are similar shots in my film *Into the Dark*: see Chapter 9.) As the anaesthetic kicks in, we see the light above the operating table from behind one (very large and translucent) eyelid. As it closes, we drift off into abstraction, and then to the heavenly trial where Peter's fate will be decided. In the cartoon short *Greedy for Tweety* (Friz Freleng, 1957) a similar behind-the-eyelid shot in a similar hospital setting is used to show Sylvester's drugged point of view as his bulldog antagonist approaches with a wooden club and malicious intent. Seen from inside, Sylvester's eyelid opens and closes and opens again before finally closing to a moment of black, followed by a graphic explosion of damage and pain.

With its thousands of drawings on cel and paper, *His Mother's Voice* is clearly an animated film. But just as clearly it is neither a cartoon nor a comedy. Kathy Easdale's voice makes the evidence of trauma all too real; it is a documentary based on a mother's bearing witness. But it is also staged as a drama, albeit one in which the resolution—the fact that Matthew is dead—is known from both the prologue and the interviewer's question. There is none of the suspense, the evocation of unease, for which the subjective point of view is used in other films. Except for the one mirror shot—the car's rear view mirror in which only Kathy's eyes are visible—Part 1 maintains a strictly subjective point of view, while the action cuts quite rapidly in time and space. And any evidence from other witnesses, even where we see their lips moving, is heard only from Kathy. Like the design—dramatic shots lit in a harsh but colourful chiaroscuro—the music is scored heavily and without any other sound.

Propelled by the "invisible force" of Kathy's narrative, Part 1 moves constantly forward in its narrative. In the literal sense, the whole of Part 2 is a flashback to the recording of the interview which we have just seen dramatized from Kathy's point of view as narrator in Part 1. Only now, in Part 2—as this new visualization of the interview unfolds in real time—is there time for the audience to reflect on what they have just seen in Part 1, identical in voice but very different in every other way. There are two mirrors in Part 2 (in the bathroom and in Matthew's bedroom) but neither shows the identity of the person behind the camera's point of view. This absence is amplified because this time, like the primitive cinema's "phantom ride" but unlike Part 1, the point of view is not recognized or addressed by anyone except the old family dog.

The movement and motivation of the shot are deliberately mysterious; the point of view seems able to roam freely about the house and yard. Like the drunken subjective point of view in Murnau's *The Last Laugh* (1924), it whirls around the backyard clothes line, falls over and gets to its feet before heading back into the house. Finally, the point of view inserts itself in the space between Kathy and the interviewer, and moves towards Kathy's lips for the *coup de grace* as she speaks the words of the ambulance man: "We're sorry, but he's passed away".

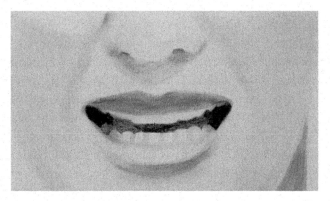

*

In presenting *His Mother's Voice* at festivals, classes, and conferences, two questions are always asked. First: why did you play the interview audio twice? I have addressed this question in the discussion above. And second: has Kathy Easdale seen the film, and what does she think of it? The answer is: I don't know, so I don't know.

When the film was completed in 1997, I sent a VHS tape to Kathy with a note inviting her to call me any time. She contacted me to say that she had received the tape, but wasn't sure when she would be able to look at it. Since then the film has screened on national television several times and at film festivals, and has been discussed in many books and journals. It has not been available online. Kathy's (missing) reaction to the film feels entirely appropriate to *His Mother's Voice*. The film is full of absence. As the credits make clear, both parts are imagined and then made as an animated film production—with storyboard, production design, animation, performance, music, and sound—but built around the only actual documentary elements in the film: Kathy's extraordinary voice and the story she tells. Most of all *His Mother's Voice* is, like the story told by his mother's voice, about the absence of Matthew.

*

Chronologically, my two early cartoons were followed by two animated documentaries. Though the subject (death) is the same, the treatments are very different. Fictional humour, however morbid, has given way to serious accounts of personal experience, each with the voice of the eyewitness narrator—one written and narrated by myself, the other taken directly from a radio interview with someone I had talked with but never met.

The visual flexibility of animation—the freedom to use very different graphic and cinematic styles in the same film—was matched by the narrative possibilities of fiction and the reality of documentary. With my interest in writing scripts that mixed live action and animation, and my interest in live action film making generally, the development of a hybrid approach to animation and film was probably inevitable.

NOTES

1 https://en.wikipedia.org/wiki/His_Master%27s_Voice retrieved 22-10-20.

2 Chion, Michel. *The Voice in Cinema*. New York: Columbia University Press, 1999. 132.

3 ibid. 133.

4 Renov, Michael quoted in: Torre, Dan. *Animation – Process, Cognition and Actuality*. New York: Bloomsbury Academic, 2017. 189.

5 Chion, Michel: op. cit. 21.

6 ibid. 17.

7 ibid. 46–47.

8 *Remembrance of Things Past*, quoted in: ibid. 46.

9 "He'll Have to Go" written by Joe & Audrey Allison, RCA Capitol, 1959.

10 Chion, Michel: op. cit. 28 (italics in original).

11 Kriger, Judith. *Animated Realism: A Behind-the-Scenes Look at the Animated Documentary Genre*. Waltham, MA: Focal Press, 2012. 120.

12 ibid. 120.

13 Barthes, Roland. *Image-Music-Text*. New York: Hill and Wang, 1977. 181 (italics in original).

14 ibid. 182, 185 (italics in original).

15 quoted in: Chion, Michel: op. cit. 118.

16 https://en.wikipedia.org/wiki/Phantom_ride retrieved 14-5-20.

17 Quoted in: Bordwell, David. *Narration in the Fiction Film*. London: Methuen, 1985. 111.

CHAPTER 8

Hybrids of Life and Death

Certain, 'tis certain; very sure, very sure: death, as the Psalmist saith, is certain to all; all shall die. How a good yoke of bullocks at Stamford fair?

WILLIAM SHAKESPEARE: *HENRY IV,*
PART TWO. ACT 3, SC 2.[1]

After the two animated documentaries I made several (mostly live action) documentaries for television, all stories about the lives of others: *Taringa 4068: Our Place and Time* (2003), *Silly and Serious: William Robinson and Self Portraits (2008),* and *La première interview/The First Interview* (2011). These films use many elements of the conventional documentary as discussed earlier. But wherever possible only the subjects are interviewed; I avoid contributions from friends or colleagues, commentators or experts, either on or off screen.

In *The First Interview,* the late French director Agnès Varda narrates a script based on extensive research, written by me in English and then translated into French. The film backgrounds and then

DOI: 10.1201/9781003199663-8

re-stages the 1886 Paris interview by the great photographer Nadar with the famous scientist Chevreul on his 100th birthday, using the original transcript as recorded in shorthand and published with the photographs in a magazine of the day. Originally planned as animation, using motion capture and CGI to give Nadar's original photographs the animated "illusion of life", the prohibitive expense of this technique for a short film required a switch to live action with actors. As produced and screened on Australian and French television, the film uses prosthetics and various post-production visual effects to produce a photographic fantasy. Like animation, it is obviously not real, for this scratchy and damaged "impossible movie" purports to be an interview on film with synchronized sound from 1886, years before the Lumière cinématographe and decades before *The Jazz Singer*. Although it uses little frame-by-frame animation in the conventional sense, *The First Interview* uses various techniques to produce a hybrid form of cinema.

Hybrid films of various types have a rich history in animation. It could be said that any animated documentary is already a hybrid of animation technique and documentary subject matter. There are also hybrids of animated and live action material, and of various animation techniques. Once seen, who can forget the truly *living* eyes in the otherwise puppet stop-motion *Madame Tutli-Putli* (Lavis/ Szczerbowski, 2007) or the disturbingly real mouths using the patented "Syncro-Vox" lip sync system in the old TV series *Clutch Cargo* with its plentiful dialogue and extremely limited (and therefore cheap) animation?[2] And then there are all the possibilities of narrative itself, as suggested by Terry Eagleton's description of the novel: "It is less a genre than an anti-genre. It cannibalizes other literary modes and mixes the bits and pieces promiscuously together".[3] In animation this promiscuity extends into the graphic and the cinematic.

The filmed work of the vaudeville "lightning sketch" artists is some of the earliest animated films. In his first film, *Little Nemo* (1911), Winsor McCay uses a live action staged "documentary" to frame the fantastic animation to follow. He tells a group of laughing and sceptical friends how he will make 4,000 drawings and deliver an animated film within a month. "McCay's new 'act' was really his old 'quick-sketch' act with the addition of the *Little Nemo* film".[4] By 1914, with *Gertie the Dinosaur*, McCay incorporated an entire element of character animation into his vaudeville act. On stage he summoned Gertie from the cartoon cave projected on the theatre's screen. He interacted with the childish, troublesome and easily upset dinosaur, and was finally borne away by her in triumph at the end of the performance. As in much theatre, of course, this integrated performance required the audience's willing suspension of disbelief. Released as a film with a live action framing story, McCay's remarkable skill conveyed the size and power of the dinosaur, and the conviction of Gertie's personality, ensuring its success then and now.

John and Faith Hubley used the unscripted voices of their young children at play to provide the narration for *Moonbird* (1959). But the images and animation skills are those of adults, creating a world that we see (or remember) as the children's fantasy. Even earlier, the live action *A Matter of Life and Death* made a fictional romantic fantasy from true if sometimes unlikely elements: an opening shot of the universe ("Big, isn't it?"), an airman's survival after jumping from a plane without a parachute,[5] hallucinations from a brain injury cured by a risky operation, a camera obscura, a fatal motorcycle accident, and others. Backed by Powell's research—though not appreciated at the time of *AMOLAD*'s release—such fantasy elements as the film's life-or-death "trial" and its "stairway to heaven" have more recently been seen as Powell seems to have intended them: as subjective representations of brain pathology in the hallucinating mind, as well as poetically and mythically symbolic images.[6] How else to explain the "timeless" scene of the naked boy-piper minding his goats, the pilot's very strange first encounter when he washes up on an English beach? The rotoscoped *Waking Life* (Linklater, 2001) can also be seen as a "waking dream" or a "waking death" or even as a hybrid narrative of life and death that flits from one reality to another.

The animated *Into the Dark* is based on my own experiences with life and death. But later, in *Chainsaw* and the later films, the hybrid form—or more accurately a hybrid of both form and technique— can encompass animation with archival films and a strange experience that is both visionary and real. The hybrid becomes a way to mix many elements into a synthesis of fact and fiction, dream and reality, past and present—one that can double and split, circle and echo, puzzle and sometimes bewilder, but that remains a human narrative of life and death.

NOTES

1 Enright, D.J. (ed) op. cit. 36.
2 Torre, Dan. *Animation – Process, Cognition and Actuality.* New York: Bloomsbury Academic, 2017. 156–158.
3 Quoted in: Alison, Jane. *Meander, Spiral, Explode: Design and Pattern in Narrative.* New York: Catapult, 2020. 12.
4 Canemaker, John. op. cit. 134.
5 Survival of Flight Sergeant Nicholas Alkemade (1944) https://en. wikipedia.org/wiki/Nicholas_Alkemade.
6 Broadbent Friedman, Diane. *A Matter of Life and Death: The Brain Revealed by the Mind of Michael Powell.* Bloomington, IN: AuthorHouse, 2008.

CHAPTER 9

Into the Dark (2001)

The past is never dead. It's not even past.

WILLIAM FAULKNER: *REQUIEM FOR A NUN*[1]

In 2000, following the success of the *Swimming Outside the Flags* animated anthology series (including *The Heat, The Humidity*), a similar call for submissions was made by the broadcaster (SBS Independent) and both state and federal funding bodies.[2] Animators were asked for short film ideas based on the idea of "home" for a series titled *Home Movies*. More than 35 years after leaving the house in Darra at the age of 14, it was still "home" to me. Having written *The Darra Dogs* 10 years before, and with the death of my father in 1998, the recording of memories of my childhood home in Darra had become both more urgent and more complicated. The new film, *Into the Dark*, would try to combine childhood memory with adult observation and speculation into a hybrid of fiction and non-fiction narratives, both animated and both dealing with nothingness and death. My mother would die in 2001, before the film was completed.

Into the Dark begins with a slow Brahms piano piece and a title graphic that moves slowly away. We are quickly thrown into a moving corridor with skewed walls and doorways: one continuous

DOI: 10.1201/9781003199663-9

shot of sketchy drawings that roll up into the ceiling and a series of lights racing past overhead.

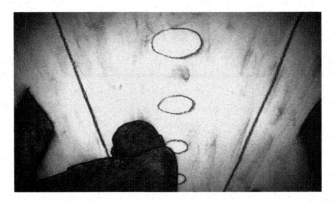

The music has gone, replaced by the urgent reassuring voices and crashing doors, the squeaking wheels and groans, of a hospital emergency. Now we hear a calm voice—adult and male, and sounding like the patient whose rolling point of view we have just witnessed—that calmly takes up the story.

It's getting dark.

Out of the blurred ceiling looms a still photograph.

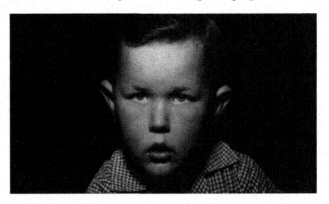

It is not the radio that introduces the interviewer and then Kathy Easdale as the narrator in *His Mother's Voice*, but the eyes of a young boy in a sepia photograph. As we zoom back, he stares at the camera, open-mouthed but intent—and surrounded by darkness.

> I can see it now. All those years ago. It's getting dark at home. Back in Darra.

We cut to a house at dusk, its windows bright, with birds flying into the darkness of the trees. There is no music, only the evening sounds of the birds and muted voices and dinner being prepared. (We called it "tea" in the working-class suburb of Darra.) For the moment all is calm. As the narrator, I describe how the light would fade quickly now and how colours would seem to flare up and glow momentarily before sinking deeper into the gloom. As in *The Darra Dogs* I am relying on my memory of those long-ago evenings, standing barefoot in the damp grass. But there are no dogs to be seen, only the sparrows flying into the grapefruit tree silhouetted against the sky.

Like *His Mother's Voice* the film has two distinct points of view in two narratives: one rendered in bright flat colours, the other in a sketchy sepia monochrome. This time, however, the stories (from a boy and a man) have very different soundtracks. And they are not presented serially, as in *His Mother's Voice*, but are intercut in an irregular rhythm that follows the events in both parts. The boy shoots birds and later, in the bathroom, tries to feel "nothing".

The man is in a medical emergency, groaning and wordless as he begins to hallucinate and later dies in the operating theatre, surrounded by shimmering animals who are trying to save him. The boy and the man may be the same person—the theme, the images of birds and the male narrator strongly imply a common experience—but there is no explicit link of name or identity.

The boy's point of view is clearly that of the narrator—in this case me—speaking as the first person "I" in a conventional voice-over: "I wait under the tree with my air rifle. I'm looking for one bird". Visually, the boy's shots are not exclusively from a subjective "I-am-a-camera" view, as they are in both parts of *His Mother's Voice*. (We see the boy waiting and his feet walking, but also his point of view as he aims his air rifle.) Later, in the bathroom, as he tries to feel "nothing" he is also stepping inside:

> ...the space of a camera obscura, its enclosedness, its darkness, its separation from an exterior (which) incarnate Descartes' 'I will now shut my eyes, I shall stop my ears, I shall disregard my senses'. The orderly and calculable penetration of light rays through the single opening of the camera corresponds to the flooding of the mind by the light of reason.[3]

The boy is innocent of Descartes and Locke, but he is *reasoning*, feeling his way in the dark towards a comprehension of death, of the bird he has just killed under the grapefruit tree. And later, in the dying man's last moments of reverie, as the boy rises from the tree, he will open his eyes and be flooded by the dazzling white light of death.

Throughout the hospital sequences the man's point of view is entirely subjective: a corridor ceiling seen from a hurtling gurney, a hairy arm, an abstract shape in a passing doorway... all strange and becoming stranger. There are no mirrors to reveal—or fail to reveal—the person through whose eyes we look and whose mind we inhabit, as there are in *His Mother's Voice* and *Lady in the Lake*. But after light floods into the mind's camera obscura, we are left with the boy's eyes in the photograph: the same eyes that have just closed forever, along with the subjective view and the man's consciousness. In the image the boy's eyes are open and intent, but as a photograph they are temporally fixed and dead.

As Bazin says: "We do not die twice. In this respect, a photograph does not have the power of a film; it can only represent someone dying or a corpse, not the elusive passage from one to another".[4] Beginning and ending with the same photograph, and by using animation rather than live action, *Into the Dark* uses both memory and speculation in a hybrid form to suggest what this passage might be like. Like *The Darra Dogs*, the "childhood" part of *Into the Dark* is set in the Brisbane suburb of Darra, and uses my own memories. But this time I am the human shooting the poor animal, rather than hating the priest for doing so. I look down at the bird's bloody breast, glowing red in the rapidly fading light of early evening.

Now that it is dead I wonder: "Does it feel nothing? What *is* nothing?"

But evening is also bath time. As a child in the bright yellow bathroom I seek to investigate further the experience of nothingness: first by holding my breath underwater to the point of blacking out, and then by jumping up in the air. I am naked and airborne, with eyes closed and hands over my ears, with "no senses at all".

I remember trying, as a child, to experience what was life and beyond life—*after* life—as the dead bird might have experienced it. And these, the moments before and during and after death, are also what the dying man in the hospital experiences.

In her book *All the Things I Lost in the Flood*, Laurie Anderson describes her mother's last words:

> She began to talk about her life and as she spoke the sentences began to fracture until she was talking in short disconnected phrases to the animals that seemed to have gathered on the ceiling.... She's talking in a high new voice I've never heard before. 'Why are there so many animals on the ceiling now?' she says.... She spoke to them tenderly. 'All you animals, ' she said... 'Tell the animals... tell all the animals...' she said.[5]

In his final days my father also saw creatures—in his case spiders—on the walls of Intensive Care, and would point them out to us.

I have no belief in a literal after-life; it appears in *Please Don't Bury Me* only because the film is a (cartoon) illustration of the humorous John Prine song. (And in my interpretation it's a cinematic heaven, with the "Paradise" theatre and a crowd of movie star "angels" led by Buster Keaton.) Otherwise, in several films I refuse to go beyond the last moment of life, of thought, of dream—however strange, a moment we will all experience in some form when the time comes. After surviving a heart attack when he was clinically dead for 6 minutes, the Australian billionaire Kerry Packer famously told an interviewer: "Son, I've been to the other side, and let me tell you, there's nothing there".[6]

Dostoyevsky[7] and the philosopher Maurice Blanchot[8] have both left accounts of facing a firing squad (in 1849 and 1944 respectively) and of their lives being spared at the last moment. There is a vast literature in fiction—speculative as it must be—addressing those last moments of life that *do* end in death. In "The Moment of Death in Modern Fiction", Robert Detweiler discusses many works by Flannery O'Connor, Hemingway, Faulkner, Borges, Cortazar, and others.[9]

Ambrose Bierce's story of the American Civil War, "An Occurrence at Owl Creek Bridge" (1891),[10] was filmed as a live action short by Robert Enrico in 1962. It has the simple shape of an adventure story and recalls the survival stories of Dostoevsky and Blanchot. A man called Peyton Farquhar stands on a bridge above Owl Creek, a rope around his neck. Facing certain death, he remembers how he came to this situation. But the rope breaks as he falls, he plunges into the water, and manages to make his escape. He finds his way back to his wife, but here the story ends quickly:

> (She) stands waiting, with a smile of ineffable joy, an attitude of matchless grace and dignity.… As he is about to clasp her, he feels a stunning blow upon the back of the neck; a blinding white light blazes all about him with a sound like the shock of a cannon—then all is darkness and silence! Peyton Farquhar was dead; his body, with a broken neck, swung gently from side to side beneath the timbers of the Owl Creek bridge.[11]

The whole escape story has happened in an extended moment that remains unexplained, and is inexplicable except in the human imagination and its capacity for hope. Farquhar's yearning for life, and to see his wife again, has been satisfied. But Bierce's brutally succinct ending provides no hope for a further continuation of Farquhar's consciousness, and certainly not an afterlife or anything else but "darkness and silence".

Tobias Wolff's story "Bullet in the Brain", discussed earlier in another context, ends in the mind of the fatally amused Anders, even as the bank robber's bullet crashes slowly through his brain. Wolff gives his character one last extended reverie, which ends in the last words of the story:

> The bullet is already in the brain…. That can't be helped. But for now Anders can still make time. Time for the shadows to lengthen on the grass, time for the tethered dog to bark at the flying ball, time for the boy in the right field to smack his sweat-blackened mitt and softly chant, *They is, they is, they is.*[12]

In "The Night Face Up", Julio Cortazar (1914–1984) begins the story with a motorcyclist and his machine speeding through a modern city—there is an accident, a hospital—and ends on the bloody steps of an Aztec temple in another time.[13] Throughout the story the motor cyclist goes back and forth between various realities (all of them dreamlike) though he remains the same person, with the same confused consciousness:

> He smelled death, and when he opened his eyes he saw the blood- soaked figure of the executioner-priest coming towards him with the stone knife in his hand. He managed to close his eyelids again, although he knew now he was not going to wake up, that he was awake, that the marvellous dream had been the other, absurd as all dreams are—a dream in which he was going through the strange avenues of an astonishing city, with green and red light that burned without fire or smoke, on an enormous metal insect that whirred away between his legs. In the infinite lie of the dream, they had also picked him up off the ground, someone had approached him also

with a knife in his hand, approached him who was lying face up, face up with his eyes closed between the bonfires on the steps.[14]

In his humble print workshop in Mexico City, José Guadalupe Posada (1852–1913) made images of death and everyday violence. Best-known for his broadside *calaveras*—skulls and skeletons at work and play in an extended dance of death—Posada's was a popular art that covered many subjects of Mexican life and death. "Like much popular art, broadside prints were only one element in a complex, hybrid discourse. There was no separation of spheres. Insofar as one code dominated the others, it was the abstract code of the narrative, which was realized in different, simultaneous modes".[15] Posada is a powerful link in the tradition that joins the pre-Columbian world to the Mexican muralists of the 20th century (Rivera, Orozco et al) and, later still, the motorcyclist in Cortazar's story.

The dying man in *Into the Dark* is also "face up" on the hospital gurney as it crashes through doors and into the calm evenings of his childhood, recollected with the piano music of Johannes Brahms. In the operating theatre he sees the doctors and nurses as birds and dogs—not pets or victims but anthropomorphic figures still trying desperately to keep their patient alive, and failing.

Finally, in a partial reversal of the anthropomorphism common in animation, the boy rises from the branch into the air. As his spread arms sweep down to his side, the drawn boy begins to fly.

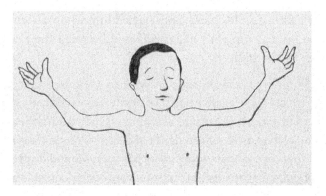

We zoom in towards him; his eyes stare out at us, widening in wonder and surprise at something—or nothing. But we never see what he sees. The frontal charcoal drawing of the boy's eyes dissolves into a photograph: the eyes of the same frontal photograph of me as a child that begins the film.

As we zoom out from these eyes (my eyes) *Into the Dark* ends with the same studio photograph of me that was at the last moment left out of *The Darra Dogs*. (A return of the repressed, perhaps, but still leaving out my brothers. Removed from this image of the studio portrait, they are invisible in the darkness surrounding me.) One generally favourable review saw the presence of this one photograph as an unnecessary step away from pure animation:

> ...*Into the Dark* is demanding, placing the viewer in an intensely subjective position while feeling at all times that this is someone else's life. On second viewing I was less than happy with the use of the photograph with its suggestion of biographical reality and of time long past. The animation can stand on its own without this.[16]

This illustrates one of the risks in hybrid storytelling: that different narratives and forms—in this case the hand-made animated drawings with their own reality and time, and the single photographic moment sliced from quotidian reality—may weaken and not strengthen each other. It's true that these two forms have very different histories and are made in different ways. But they also share a great deal: the frame, the shot, the cut, coherent and organized movement—in the case of the photograph, the camera movement of a zoom—all serving a narrative, cinematic purpose. And *Into the Dark* has only one (male, adult) voice, implying some connection between the boy, with the male narrator's voice in the first person, and the man in the hospital. The photograph's "suggestion of biographical reality and of time long past" is exactly what is intended.

Into the Dark shows a boy shooting birds and a man near death, with an uncertain number of years between. Only the boy has a coherent voice: the voice of a man speaking with the voice of memory, in the present tense. Who else is the narrator if not the man whose groaning "voice" is heard in the sketchy hospital scenes? To be clear and obvious I might have begun *Into the Dark* with the words: "This is me as a child". Or with the words that begin Chris Marker's *La Jetée* (1962): "This is the story of a man marked by an image of his childhood".[17]

Beginning with a boy's point of view as he witnesses a man's death at Orly airport in Paris, *La Jetée* is a short film about memory and death—and photography. "Moments to remember are just like other moments. They are only made memorable by the scars they leave". (In the opening titles, the film is explicitly termed "un photo-roman": "a photo-novel".) Marker uses not one photograph but many to tell a story of speculative fiction. In the "present" (a blasted Paris after World War III) a man is sent back into the past and ahead into the future; the underground experimenters hope to find help there. In the past the man remains himself and meets a woman. Over a series of meetings they are attracted to each other and are happy together, especially in a museum full of stuffed animals and birds. On old stone walls they see chalk graffiti drawings of names and love-hearts, but also ancient and deeply incised skulls and crossbones. The film's one moment of cinematic life (several seconds of live action) is a look by the woman, lying in bed, towards the camera, with the sound of massed birds on the soundtrack.

In noting its use of so many stills shot on the *banc titre* (animation stand) Chris Darke is in no doubt: "*La Jetée* is an animation".[18] And after considering the many ways in which the film's images occupy a "hybrid state somewhere between photography and film, stillness and movement", he settles for the term "visions".[19] The American critic Ernest Callenbach, who discussed the film with Marker himself, denies that it is either romantic or science fiction. "The overwhelming point of *La Jetée* is the simple, awesome difference between being alive and being dead".[20]

When the man and the woman look at a cross-section of an ancient tree, with time and history inscribed in a once-living thing, they echo the scene in Hitchcock's *Vertigo* (1958) when Madeleine responds to Scottie: "I don't like it. Knowing I have to die". At the end of *La Jetée*, after all his tortured and marvellous adventures in time and space and memory, the man is back at Orly airport.

> On this hot Sunday before the war, where he could now stay, he realized that the child he had once been must be there too, watching the planes. But first he looked for the woman's face, at the end of the jetty. He ran towards her. But when he saw the man from the underground camp he realized that one cannot escape time, and that this haunted moment, given him to see as a child, was the moment of his own death.

Most films end with a fade to black. In theatrical terms it is like the lights fading or the curtain coming down. On stage and screen, it is also the end of the performance—the experience as scripted by the writer, impersonated by the players, and organized by the technicians. To the extent that the performance is an illusion of life, this is a kind of death. But in a cinema the actors are not there to hear the applause or to take a curtain call. The lights go up to reveal an emptying room with desultory activity and muted sounds.

The man in *Into the Dark* is slowly enveloped in—embraced by—his own memories. He begins with action and drama, surrounded by other adults in the hospital. Each time he remembers his childhood, he returns calmer, more removed from the life-and-death drama around him. Perhaps he realizes that his childish thoughts about life and death are a consolation after all. The birds he shot, like the dogs he saw at play and dead in *The Darra Dogs*, are still alive within him. The nothingness he contemplated is inhabited by these creatures; finally he becomes one of them. The film ends, as it began, with sketchy animated drawings and the photograph of the child—a moment of life, a slab of death—and then a final fade to black.

*

In June 1983 we were staying with an animation fan and his family in a large house in the wealthy Paris suburb of Neuilly. Our host arranged a visit to the office of Argos Films, which was nearby.

I was shown into a large windowless video edit suite—the standard 1980s array of video monitors and control panels with illuminated buttons—and introduced to Chris Marker. He was tall, I think (though not as tall as me) and slim, totally bald and dressed in shirt and slacks: all in black. He spoke good English and said he had seen my film *Dance of Death* and had enjoyed it. (A TV screening in France was possible because the film had won the Jury Prize at the Annecy festival just a few days before.) I have only this one image of his face and figure in that room, a wide shot, though we must have been closer when introduced. But, of course, there are very few photographic images of Marker with which to compare my memory. I remember no-one else in the room, nor anything else we discussed. Marker's film *Sans Soleil (Sunless)* was released that year. The title always reminds me of that video edit suite without windows. Perhaps he was working on it; perhaps we even discussed it. I don't remember.

NOTES

1 Faulkner, William. *Requiem for a Nun*. Harmondsworth, Middlesex: Penguin, 1967. 81.
2 Torre, Dan and Lienors Torre. *Australian Animation: An International History*. Cham, Switzerland: Palgrave Macmillan, 2018. 230–231.
3 Crary, Jonathan. *Techniques of the Observer: On Vision and Modernity in the Nineteenth Century*. Cambridge, MA: MIT Press, 1992. 43.
4 Quoted in: Combs, C. Scott. *Deathwatch: American Film, Technology and the End of Life*. New York: Columbia University Press, 2014. 14–15.
5 Anderson, Laurie. *All the Things I Lost in the Flood*. New York: Rizzoli Electa, 2018. 272.
6 https://www.theguardian.com/news/2005/dec/28/guardianobituaries.cricket retrieved 4-3-2020.
7 Dostoevsky, Fyodor. "Letter to his brother 23-12-1849" quoted in: https://www.usrepresented.com/2014/02/02/dostoevsky/ retrieved 5-3-20.
8 Blanchot, Maurice. *The Instant of My Death*. and Derrida, Jacques. *Demeure: Fiction and Testimony*. Stanford, CA: Stanford University Press, 2000. 5–7.
9 Detweiler, Robert. "The Moment of Death in Modern Fiction". University of Wisconsin Press: *Contemporary Literature* (13:3, Summer 1972). 269–294.
10 Bierce, Ambrose. *In the Midst of Life and Other Tales*. New York: New American Library, 1961. 16–26.
11 ibid. 25–26.
12 Wolff, Tobias. op. cit. 268 (italics in original).
13 in: Cortazar, Julio. *The End of the Game and Other Stories*. New York: Harper Colophon, 1978. 66–76.
14 ibid. 76
15 Rothenstein, Julian (ed). *J.G Posada: Messenger of Mortality*. London: Redstone Press, 1989. 22.
16 Gallasch, Keith. "The View from the Child". *Realtime 51*, Oct–Nov 2002 http://www.realtimearts.net/article/issue51/6875 retrieved 5-3-20.
17 The original narration and graphics in *La Jetée* are in French; the whispers or background murmurs are in German.
18 Darke, Chris. *La Jetée*. London: BFI & Palgrave, 2016. 73–74.
19 ibid. 63.
20 ibid. 53.

CHAPTER 10

Chainsaw (2007)

We read the letters of the dead like helpless gods,
but gods, nonetheless, since we know the dates that follow…

WISŁAWA SZYMBORSKA—
"THE LETTERS OF THE DEAD"[1]

Despite the years of film-making and animation, the archivist in me had never really gone away. For years I collected material about the famous Australian rodeo bull "Chainsaw" and Luis Miguel Dominguin, the great Spanish bullfighter. My interest in both of them began with reports of their deaths.

In May 1996 Melbourne's *The Age* newspaper carried an obituary of the famous Spanish bullfighter Luis Miguel Dominguin with the headline: "Spain's greatest matador lays down his sword".[2]

DOI: 10.1201/9781003199663-10

With accounts of his many "kills" and injuries, the obituary detailed his affair with Ava Gardner during her marriage to Frank Sinatra. There was also Dominguin's own description, quoted earlier, of why he fought bulls: "It is like being with your lover when her husband comes in with a gun. The bull is the woman, the husband, and the pistol—all in one. No other life can give you all that". Alongside a photograph of a young and "impossibly handsome" Dominguin with his wife (the Italian film star Lucia Bosè), their children, and his friend Pablo Picasso, this strikingly romantic description of adultery and machismo was worth keeping on file.

Early in 1997 a smaller obituary appeared in Brisbane's *Courier Mail*, celebrating the life of a bull called Chainsaw: "Australia's greatest bucking bull dies".[3]

Under a head shot of the celebrated bull, the journalist Oscar Kornyei gives a wry but respectful account of Chainsaw's peerless record against the best rodeo bull riders; only six ever rode him for the required eight seconds. His owner admits to having "tears in my eyes" when told that the (then retired) bull would have to be put down. "He used to jump up so high you could almost run underneath him if you were quick enough. At the Port Macquarie rodeo they gave Chainsaw a minute's silence". I kept this clipping too. Already there was a link between the Man and the Bull.

> Apart from the headlines and their status as obituaries, the two news stories were oddly similar: a man and a bull in an obviously violent and dangerous situation that was also artificial, metaphorical and somehow—at least for the humans involved, and whatever its moral dimensions—poetic. At this stage the two 'bull' stories seemed to have little in common with the mechanical tool known as the chainsaw. But research might show otherwise. Already I felt that there would be many more stories, and that they might form a 'chain' of some sort. Several years later I started to research the lives and careers of Dominguin and Chainsaw. Both were dead of course. Chainsaw had never been interviewed, though a documentary had been made about the great bull and those who tried to ride him: *Chainsaw: Bull Born Bad* (Shirley Barrett, 1991).[4]

The fictional elements of *Chainsaw* also required extensive research. As well as the very different traditions of the bullfight and the rodeo, there were many chainsaw safety videos to be viewed, and the extensive lore of the chainsaw itself in popular culture as an instrument of sudden and often fatal violence, in fact and in fiction. The research for *Chainsaw* included seeing one bullfight in the most celebrated arena in Spain, where Dominguin had often appeared: Las Ventas in Madrid.

In her book *Animated Realism*, Judith Kriger describes *Chainsaw* as "an award-winning chain of linked stories, driven by human dreams and fantasies, romance and machismo... an inventive part-fact, part-fiction hybrid".[5] *Chainsaw* is a hybrid not only in its storytelling and narrative structure but also in the design and techniques used in the film's production. Along with available archival photographic material, both moving and still, animation offers a vast choice of graphic approaches to the representation of reality—in this case a reality of human rituals and romance infused with sex and violence.

Chainsaw uses several types of what might loosely be called "documentary" styles. First there is the sponsored film: a chainsaw safety video in which an expert (Frank Gardner) shows us the right way to do things. "Chainsaw: Working Safe #17" is a product of the 1980s, with plenty of cheesy elements to match its smeared video and chunky yellow graphics: the "professional" voice over, the vacuous library music, the lame attempts at humour, the limited performance range of the willing amateurs Frank and his wife Ava.

But it's also full of excellent safety advice, and its intentions are good. Second, there is the old-style cinema newsreel with scripted voice over and blaring music; and third, the modern television news story with voice over and interviews (phone/audio or video) for background and context, and its vast resources of historical footage and stills.

Between them, these two "news" approaches cover the needs of the two obituaries: Chainsaw the bull and Dominguin the man. The fact that almost all of this material is animated does, of course, bring into question its status as documentary. But all the information sounds—and is, according to my research—factually correct. *Chainsaw* is also laced with film stars and bull fights in black and white archival live action that is certainly real as cinematic documentary.

The world inhabited by *Chainsaw's* fictional characters is designed to be both believable and consistent with that of the documentary, while remaining convincing and entertaining as drama. There is a constant leakage of story elements from fiction to documentary and back again, and changes in behaviour over time and in different roles. In fiction, the passion in Frank and Ava's marriage has cooled over the years since the safety video was shot; their house and yard, once pretty with a green lawn and garden, are now bare and run-down. Hard at work in the bush, Frank now ignores all those rules about chainsaw safety he once promoted so avidly.

But things have also changed in the world of fact. Both Chainsaw the bull and Dominguin the bullfighter are dead, of course. And not only them. For the information of the living audience—the Polish poet Szymborska's "helpless gods"—at the end of *Chainsaw* are listed the birth and death dates of all four real characters who are represented in the film. First are the three humans who once formed that famous "eternal triangle": still together in this animated film, in death as in life. "Frank Sinatra 1915–1998, Ava Gardner 1922–1990, Luis Miguel Dominguin 1926–1996". On the next title card, at a respectful distance and alone, comes the bull: "Chainsaw 1981–1996". There is often laughter in the audience at this moment of comic incongruity, a nod to one of Monro's ten classes of humour: "importing into one situation what belongs in another".[6] A newspaper's obituary for a rodeo bull is also a comic element in Kornyei's original *Courier Mail* article in 1996.

We know from the archival newsreel material used in *Chainsaw* that the fictional Australians Frank and Ava Gardner both have a strong romantic identification with their famous Hollywood namesakes Frank Sinatra and Ava Gardner. As the 1951 newsreel narrator says: "At a midnight film preview Frank Sinatra heads a list of film celebrities including his new wife Ava Gardner", we see the glamorous couple in a jostling crowd, talking to the comic actor Sid Caesar.

At different times we see "our" fictional and animated Frank and Ava Gardner reflected in car mirrors, *looking* quite separately at themselves but *seeing* the Hollywood Frank and Ava. In their minds the old newsreel has become a dream that for Frank now turns into a nightmare. After he discovers her adultery with Lewis, the same celebrity footage is slowed down to show Frank Gardner's new vision of his wife Ava with the face of a scheming and treacherous film star, Ava Gardner. We have just seen Ava asleep in their bed and in a fantasy of her own, unaware of the wreckage of the house around her, and that her lover Lewis has already fled in terror. She smiles and waves as she dreams of that bullfight in Spain sometime in the 1950s.

Historical and picture research has its moments of discovery when the past comes alive, quite unlike anything that animation can offer. As I say in an interview for Kriger's book:

Looking for footage of Ava Gardner, I came across footage of Gardner sitting at a bullfight and seeing a guy being gored by a bull. I couldn't believe it! It wasn't Dominguin, though he was at the same bullfight. It's an amazing piece of footage, and my favourite part of the film is seeing her face when the guy was gored because it really did happen. The movie star "mask" was gone, and you can really see the shock on her face.[7]

The black and white footage is silent and damaged, and without other information or documentation. But its power is undiminished after more than 60 years. Ava Gardner is filmed *there* at the bullfight, the glamorous movie star wearing a Spanish *mantilla*, smiling but mute as she gazes at the matadors' parade, mouthing "oh it's beautiful!" The bullfighter is gored *there*. As he is carried from the arena, the shock and horror register on Ava Gardner's face *there*. For our fictional Ava, as for our Frank, a dream has just become a nightmare. And when she later wakes up—a fictional moment we are spared—the reality will be much worse than she could have imagined.

In a film where "real" life is presented as animation via rotoscope, it seems appropriate that, outside the fantasy sequences just discussed, "archival" and therefore "real" stills and footage should also be presented as black and white illustrations and animation. In the news story of Dominguin's death, we see stills of some famous sexual conquests, a "police procedural" image of the actress Miroslava Sternova's body after her suicide "clutching a photograph of Dominguin", the funeral of Manolete the great bullfighter, then the bull that killed him, and the rotoscoped "original" of Dominguin's Hollywood screen test, with Ava Gardner feeding him lines. Some are drawn from original photographic material; others use conjecture and actors when images are unavailable. But all are based on research; even if the image was never captured on film, we believe that the event really happened.

*

Few of my films have a simple story structure. In a fictional cartoon like *Dance of Death*, events accumulate in a seemingly haphazard way, until the dark and jumbled comedy becomes fatal for the Roberts family. Although its individual stories are my childhood memories, *The Darra Dogs* is organized as a series of separate sequences without links and often without internal cause-and-effect. In this the film reflects the world of the child, at least the one that I remember in Darra. Even *His Mother's Voice*, in which Kathy Easdale tells her tragic story in such a remarkably clear way, presents the story twice—each time with a very different cinematic point of view and illustrative technique.

Jane Alison investigates the shapes that stories can take, beginning with "the famous arc" of the drama from Aristotle ("beginning, middle, and end; complication, change, dénouement") and Freytag's similar "famous triangle or pyramid", proceeding to the sexualized arc of Robert Scholes: "The fundamental orgastic rhythm of tumescence and detumescence, of tension and resolution, of intensification to the point of climax and consummation".[8] In film, Aristotle's dramatic structure has come down to us as Syd Field's template in *Screenplay*,[9] and Georges Franju's remark that "movies should have a beginning, a middle and an end" to which Jean-Luc Godard famously and mischievously (and perhaps apocryphally) replied: "certainly, but not necessarily in that order".[10]

Alison's project is to discover and describe works of fiction with structures "other than an arc, structures that create an inner sensation of travelling *toward* something and leave a shape behind, so that the stories feel *organized....* (M)any of the structures that recur in these texts coincide with fundamental patterns in nature".[11] She finds these in Peter S. Stevens' book *Patterns in Nature*, a book of descriptive natural science and mathematics with drawings, photographs, and diagrams that I remember well from the 1970s.[12] Some of her examples from fiction are based on flow (wave, meander, spiral), others on a central form (radials, explosions), and still others are networks, cells, and fractals. In her analysis of these patterns, the narratives discussed by Alison always reflect powerful human concerns rather than merely formal experimentation. "I believe they've done this organically: a meander or net or explosion was simply the pattern the material needed".[13]

One story she examines is Wolff's "Bullet in the Brain", mentioned twice earlier. (The last moments of Anders' life stretch across not only the last three pages of Wolff's short story but my discussion of three films.) At this point, the story's narrative flow pauses quite suddenly to examine along with Anders—the pistol beneath his chin forcing his eyes upwards—a mythological scene of bovine seduction painted on the ceiling of the bank. It is this scene that triggers Anders' helpless (and soon to be fatal) amusement:

> To make the cow sexy, the painter had canted her hips suggestively and given her long droopy eyelashes through which she gazed back at the bull with sultry welcome. The bull wore a smirk and his eyebrows were arched. If there'd been a bubble coming out of his mouth, it would have said, "Hubba hubba."[14]

Outside its bank robbery context, this extract reads almost like a scene from *Chainsaw*, if *Chainsaw* had been an animated cartoon with similarly anthropomorphic characters and played for laughs. In preparing to make just such a film about bullfighting—*Bully for Bugs* (1953)—Chuck Jones wanted to see the reality of the *corrida* for himself:

> (I)f I'm going to do it, why not study a little bit about it and have the fun of knowing that I'm doing a gentle take-off on something that really exists... (I) finally went down to Mexico City to see a bullfight, and it scared the hell out of me... here was this thing, it weighed 3,000 pounds, with these stilettos on either side of its head, and the only thing between it and death is a slender man... all dressed in these beautiful clothes, the suit of lights they call them.[15]

As it is, *Chainsaw* is neither a Bugs Bunny cartoon with its visual gags and verbal puns ("What a gulli-bull! What a nin-cow-poop!") nor a story about a murder during a bank robbery. (These blunt descriptions are wholly inadequate to the art of both Jones and Wolff.)

> In writing *Chainsaw*, I was confident in using a web (or chain) of interconnecting stories, even if it was not immediately obvious how they were linked, or whether they were linked at all. The film needed to entertain (amuse, fascinate, scare, horrify, disgust, charm, arouse) the audience enough so that impatience was forestalled or suspended—like the theatre's 'suspension of disbelief'—and replaced, at least for long enough, by curiosity. One might even expect that some in the audience might try to step back from the puzzle, to guess how things might turn out. In fact, some viewers of *Chainsaw*

were disappointed that they could predict aspects of the story—different aspects, it turned out—as if the film was a cat-and-mouse game between writer and viewer to spin out the surprises until the very end. Yet inevitability—both tragic and comic—is a powerful element in storytelling and the drama, as shown in the unfolding of any bullfight or eight second rodeo bull ride. The storyteller's inventiveness cannot include all options; there is always the responsibility to the material itself. This is never reducible to veering plot points or cute reveals. If they are to be effective, surprises must be embedded in what has gone before, as expressed not only in story but in characters, style, tone and all the rest.[16]

In fact, the structure of *Chainsaw* is a net or web of intersecting and overlapping triangles and interstices. They include the "eternal triangles" of Frank, Ava, and Lewis the rodeo bull rider (fiction), that of Frank Sinatra, Ava Gardner, and Luis Miguel the bullfighter (fact) and, in both rodeo bull riding and the bullfight, the essentially professional triangle of two performers (man and bull) and the crowd. There are three main life stories or threads in the film, each of which ends in the death of the protagonist: those of Chainsaw the Australian bucking bull and Dominguin the Spanish bullfighter (both factual, as revealed by the original newspaper obituaries and other research), and that of Frank Gardner the chainsaw operator and safety video performer (fiction). Each of these stories is told in a different way.

The story of Chainsaw the rodeo bull begins as a news item about his recent death, complete with a voice-over narrator and interviews with his grieving owner and Lewis Donovan, the (fictional) first man to ride him. Without any caricature or anthropomorphism, the animated Chainsaw seems very much alive and ready for any variety of bull action.

The late great Chainsaw stands grazing in a perfect Australian paddock under a cloudless blue sky, beside a great gum tree, with blue hills in the distance. A white cockatoo flies slowly across the peaceful perfect scene. A few cows graze nearby. In a phone call voice-over, Chainsaw's owner admits to having tears in his eyes when he found out that the great bull would have to be put down: "Big thing, losing him." Meanwhile old Chainsaw does what bulls do: he dumps a mound of dung on the sweet pasture, moos, then ambles off screen. (Later we will see what is on his mind, as he mounts a red cow.) Everything is calm and perfect, but unsettling: this is not the image that would normally accompany such a dramatic story. Several times Chainsaw returns to this 'heavenly' scene: bulls, birds and blue hills, with no humans in sight. Much later, as night falls, it is the last shot in the film.[17]

Already there is a link to *Chainsaw*'s second story, the timber worker Frank Gardner and his wife Ava from the chainsaw safety video that begins and ends the film: "Working Safe #17". At the first rodeo they are young and happy, and have come from their pretty "Queenslander" house and garden to see Lewis ride the great bull for the first time that day. Later, grown older and distant from each other, they are there again when the late Chainsaw is honoured with a minute's silence. Ava gazes fondly at the handsome Lewis in the row of hatless cowboys with heads bowed. Their eyes meet and they smile, as they do again later in the supermarket before their afternoon tryst.

Frank has been busy out in the bush, felling trees with his chainsaw—and without any safety equipment. He comes home early, sees and hears the house rocking with sex, and takes his revenge. Lost and flying in a haze of passion, the lovers are unaware as Frank brings the house crashing to the ground. The eternal triangle is soon resolved into its constituent parts: Lewis runs off, pursued by Frank's dog; Ava sleeps on, dreaming her Hollywood self at a bullfight that turns into horror; Frank uses his chainsaw to end his pain and join his idealized Ava in the sky.

Earlier, introducing *Chainsaw*'s third story, "we cut from a flirting close-up of Ava at the Port Macquarie rodeo to flamenco guitar and a black bull as it charges into the arena in Spain to meet his killer. The career of Luis Miguel Dominguin, a romantic who spent his lifetime with bulls, is compressed into a few minutes, and into the form of the *corrida* itself".[18] Much of the traditional bullfight—a complicated ritual, with ceremony, music, a prescribed series of manoeuvres for the man and tortures for the bull—is replaced with scenes from Dominguin's life:

his relationship with Ava Gardner and her marriage to Frank Sinatra, the suicide of another lover, his self-described moment of truth in the traditional arena with jet trails overhead.[19] But the essentials of the *corrida* remain. Without ever knowing its fate, the bull will die within the prescribed 20 minutes. Of course this is a metaphor for Fate itself, the certain future death known to every human from childhood, and certainly to Dominguin. Even with his 2,000 "kills", there is always physical and even mortal risk for the matador too. In *Chainsaw*, as in the *corrida*, the end of Dominguin's story is known. It is announced in the news voice-over at the beginning, and confirmed as the living man stands over the dead bull, to the cheers of the crowd: "Luis Miguel Dominguin, dead at 69".

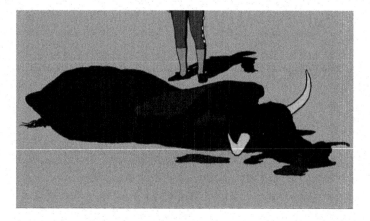

Like the bull that Dominguin kills here—and unlike the bull in *Bully for Bugs* which ostentatiously and anthropomorphically racks up Bugs Bunny as one of *his* "kills"—the animals in *Chainsaw* are always animals. Though they are bit players in the romantic and violent stories of the humans, there are several birds with important roles in providing links and continuity. The kookaburra fails to save its chicks from a tree felled by Frank's chainsaw and is then killed by his car. The crow soon eats the kookaburra as carrion beside the road. The magpie flies with a worm in its beak from Frank's doomed house to the scene of his suicide, and survives to feed its chicks. Unlike the bulls, the birds in *Chainsaw* are never the centre of attention. Birds flit and fly throughout the film—they are there in Chainsaw's sunny paddock at the start and in the twilight at the end—but they are never noticed by the humans. Most dramatically, animation allows us to fly along with the kookaburra after the death of its chicks, moving in slowly to an almost silent close-up as it glides through the blurred forest.

For a long moment we are in the bird's world of quiet flight, where only animation can take us. When the bird is hit by his car, Frank hears the impact but looks back only briefly and sees nothing.

*

After *Chainsaw* I turned back to my own life, though still in the shadow of death. And these films would still deploy various cinematic elements in different combinations of fiction and non-fiction—old Hollywood movies and a backyard photograph, rotoscope and cartoon animation, dream and self-portrait—with fantasy and reality woven through the narratives. Memory, like animation, can be both true and fantastic. Fantasy can *be* reality.

NOTES

1 Szymborska, Wislawa. *View with a Grain of Sand: Selected Poems.* Orlando: Harvest, 1995. 71.
2 Anon. "Spain's Greatest Matador Lays Down His Sword". *The Age.* Melbourne: 10-5-1996. 9.
3 Kornyei, Oscar. "Australia's Greatest Bucking Bull Dies". *The Courier Mail.* Brisbane: 9-1-1997. 3.
4 Tupicoff, Dennis. "How to Write a Screenplay with a Chainsaw". *Journal of Screenwriting,* 9:3 (2018). 280.
5 Kriger, Judith. op. cit. 125.
6 Monro, D.H. op. cit. 40.
7 in Kriger, Judith. op. cit. 127–128.
8 Alison, Jane. *Meander, Spiral, Explode: Design and Pattern in Narrative.* New York: Catapult, 2020. 10–13.
9 Field, Sid. *Screenplay: The Foundations of Screenwriting.* New York: Dell Publishing, 1979.
10 *Oxford Dictionary of Quotations.* Oxford University Press, 1999. 342.
11 Alison, Jane. op. cit. 20 (italics in original).
12 Stevens, Peter S. *Patterns in Nature.* Harmondsworth: Penguin, 1976.
13 Alison, Jane. op. cit. 247.
14 Wolff, Tobias. op. cit. 265.
15 Jones, Chuck. "What's Up, Down Under?" in: Cholodenko, Alan (ed). op. cit. 51–52.
16 Tupicoff, Dennis. "How to write a screenplay with a chainsaw" op. cit. 282–283.
17 ibid. 285–286.
18 ibid. 286.
19 Müller, Peter and Daniele Carbonel. *Costumes of Light.* New York: Assouline, 2004. 6.

CHAPTER 11

A Photo of Me (2017)

Police Captain: Who was murdered?
Frank: I was.

D.O.A. (RUDOLPH MATÉ, 1950)

I had often thought of making a film using one of the very few photographs from my childhood in Darra. There were several ideas for animated shorts based on one particular image presumably taken by my father Len (1922–1998) with our Kodak box camera.

DOI: 10.1201/9781003199663-11

It is a photo of me in a family album, a small black and white photograph with "Dennis Tupicoff" printed beside it in my mother's hand. It has no date, but must be from late 1952 or early 1953. The subject of this photograph is a toddler wearing rather worn hand-me-down clothes that my mother would have made on her Singer treadle sewing machine. But within the vertical rectangle of the frame, as with any image like this, there are other elements that contribute to its meaning.

I'm sitting on the grass beside the concrete side path and the fibro house where we lived until I was 14. My parents had bought it very cheaply as a small house across the road from a sewage dump, and had built extra rooms and paths with their own hands. The house and its large yard, which we left in 1965, had appeared as animation in both *The Darra Dogs* and *Into the Dark*. As part of the Darra reference footage for *The Darra Dogs*, I shot video of the house in 1991. It was demolished in about 2003 and was replaced by three townhouses.

The train and spinning top have obviously been placed in front of me as props, but they are strangely apt. As an adult the train would be a cornerstone of cinema for me: the Lumières' 1895 shot of the train arriving at La Ciotat, the early cinema's "phantom rides", Keaton's *The General* (1926), Konchalovsky's *Runaway Train* (1985), and so many others. In the first sequence of *Dance of Death* I would draw a speeding train that kills a mother who pushes her baby to safety—and over a cliff. Later there was an unproduced feature script called *Train to Glory*. The central mechanical element of the toy spinning top (a vertical helical shaft) was also that of the massive shaft driving the 35 mm Acme animation camera on which many of my films would be shot. Because I was so young, the "top and train" photograph was a "memory I don't remember"; this became the working title of the new film. There were other memories too. Some I remembered—like going to "the pictures" at the local movie theatre in Darra, and screaming under the rails as the Brisbane-Ipswich train passed over me.

And others I did not, but had been told about—like my ability to walk home from the pictures while fast asleep.

Since childhood I had been interested in photography, and as a film maker I had made various forms of live action as well as animation. Like *The First Interview* (2011), this new animated film would be a hybrid of documentary and fiction, a cinematic reconstruction from an archive of photographs. But it would use rotoscope animation and not live action, making a clear distinction between the few extant childhood photographs of me and the narratives of memory that were neither always my own nor completely reliable. How did I know who was in the backyard when the "top and train" photo was taken?

Had I *really* seen the Hollywood film noir *D.O.A.* at the Darra pictures in about 1959?

Our daughter Zelda, who as a child had wanted a dog (and never got one, but saw *The Darra Dogs* instead), was by 2013 a mother herself. Her son Bertie was the right age for the toddler and looked very similar to me in the 1952 image. Zelda plays my mother; I play my father; two young friends play my older brothers Gary and Ross. Like all drawn animation (even with rotoscope used as here) the images are clearly non-photographic. In bright daylight the monochrome figures stand with their strong Queensland shadows but with no background, in an expanse of pure white. At the pictures my parents and their three boys stare up at the screen, the light from *D.O.A.* reflecting on us in the dark.

Under the street light my whole family walks out of the darkness and then disappears again.

There are three main stories told in *A Photo of Me*: the taking of the photo, the scene at the Darra "pictures" (both animated), and the live action feature we are watching. Formally the film is constructed around the taking of the photograph by my father, with the help of the whole family. It begins with two earlier backyard photographs of me as a baby—the only archive up to this point (1952–1953)—and a strangely dramatic orchestral score. After the title my barefoot mother walks in front of a still and places me on the ground with my toys.

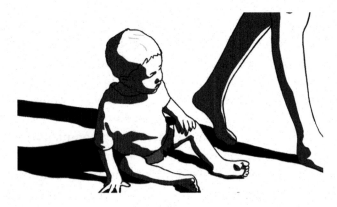

The top is already spinning; from my point of view the family is trying energetically to have me perform for the camera. As the orchestra plays, my attention is drawn towards the spinning top, then into its shiny shimmering surface, and a wobbling highlight.

As the film unfolds, the scene in the backyard comes and goes in the mind of the (now older) child as he struggles to stay awake at the Darra pictures one night in about 1959. The opening orchestral score is drawn directly from the opening sequence of *D.O.A.*, which ends as Frank meets the police captain in the Homicide office and the boy hears that startling exchange:

Police Captain: Who was murdered?
Frank: I was.

The original feature *D.O.A.* is told in one long flashback that begins and ends in the police office. It shows the existential desperation of a man who discovers he has been fatally poisoned but doesn't know why or by whom. Frank Bigelow is driven to solve the mystery and explain it to someone—to the cops, to us, to himself—before he dies. He has indeed been murdered.

For the boy the *D.O.A.* narrative comes and goes as sleep overcomes him. At first he wakes up and is startled by the fact that a murdered man—a dead man—is speaking. The policemen listen gravely to the man's story; no one is in a hurry. The boy's brothers make fun of the fact that he's now interested in such a spooky idea; they play "ghosts" in front of the screen and he is momentarily scared.

But the brothers settle down and the boy's interest fades as the flashback begins, with its inevitable expository account of Normal Life and the Love Interest of Frank and Paula as the background for the drama to come. The boy turns his head to study with some seriousness his parents—his father is smoking a cigarette—and his two brothers as they gaze at the screen. Soon, however, he is drowsy again; despite the slamming doors he has no interest in the romantic talk of this couple. There is a bar, some drinks. The boy's eyes close.

Soon he's dreaming of the backyard again, with his family throwing their arms about, and now with a jazz soundtrack. When his brother pushes the toy train, it takes the boy off into another more recent flashback. He climbs the wooden structure of a railway bridge and waits under the vibrating rails for the approaching train.

The up-tempo jazz continues as the train roars over him; he is a few inches from certain death, and screaming. He wakes up in the movie theatre to see on the screen the almost hallucinatory close-ups of the black musicians in *D.O.A.*'s nightclub scene.

The psychologist Sylvia Anthony explains this stage in childhood: "(T)he generality of death is realized.... This intellectual process is normally achieved during the period between six or seven and eleven or twelve years of age".[1] This is also the period when the child will engage in forbidden and dangerous activities. "In the dare stage, children devise a mixture of reality and fantasy in facing their fears and the challenges of life".[2] In my case this involved screaming beneath a speeding locomotive, a practice included by Anthony in her short list of childhood dares: "to put one's hand in fire, *to lie under the train*, run last across the street".[3] In fact the main physical danger was the boiling water that often splashed down from the steam locomotive as it passed over me.

At around this age I realized "the generality of death" in other ways, as described in other films: the fates of various dogs in *The Darra Dogs*, and my own shooting of birds in *Into the Dark*.

The drama of Frank Bigelow's death—one long flashback mostly from the implied point of view of the doomed man himself—is, for me as a child, another confirmation of death's inevitability and the many unexpected and imaginative ways in which life and death can be played out.

Woken by the blaring jazz, the boy sees Frank receive the doctor's grim prognosis and then the merciless summing-up: "I don't think you fully understand, Bigelow. You've been murdered". Panicked and doomed, Frank runs through the crowded streets of San Francisco. The boy's eyes close once more in sleep. With much of *D.O.A.* elided, he wakes just once more, as Frank visits a photography studio to pursue some (to the boy by now unfathomable) evidence. Frank runs from the studio energized, but the boy's head now rests in his mother's lap. By the time the first bullets fly, just a few seconds later, the boy is too deeply asleep to hear them. From now on, though we see him in the theatre, he is (in the conscious sense) absent from the film. Unlike his parents and brothers he sees neither the resolution of the story nor Frank's death.

As Frank sickens, collapses, and dies in the Homicide office, the spinning top in the backyard slows, loses its balance, and comes to a halt. With the click of the camera's shutter, the (fixed, vertical) *frame* of photographic film is exposed to that morning light. The image is *taken* from the evanescent now into the eternal present of the still photograph: "An asymbolic Death, outside of religion, outside of ritual, a kind of abrupt dive into literal Death. Life/Death: the paradigm is reduced to a single click, the one separating the initial pose from the final print".[4]

In 1865 the American poet Emily Dickinson perhaps describes a more spiritual view of photography's "decisive moment":

> The Soul's distinct connection
> With immortality
> Is best disclosed by Danger
> Or quick Calamity—

As Lightning on a Landscape
Exhibits Sheets of Place—
Not yet suspected—but for Flash—
And Click—and Suddenness.[5]

Within the frame of the photograph, time has stopped in Darra. The negative image appears in a close-up that fills the (fixed, horizontal) film frame. The film's soundtrack, still borrowed from *D.O.A.*, continues.

Captain: Call the morgue.

As arrangements are made in the office, the still turns to positive and the shot widens until we see the (fixed, vertical) edges of the image and the shadow of the child behind it. Now my mother, still rotoscoped, returns to lift me up from behind the photo and bears me away.

Captain: Better make it "Dead On Arrival".

Set in the stark white backyard as before, the photo is a vertical photographic portrait of me with the top and the train. All three objects (the top, the train, and me) have been seen earlier as rotoscope drawings with black shadows, moving in dramatic monochrome with no background or frame other than the film frame itself. Now there is a background: the concrete path and the house, the scrappy grass and dirt on which I've been placed. And everywhere there are the myriad details of photographic reality missing from its animated re-enactment: the loose threads of my shirt, the blades of grass, the plants in the garden bed between the path and the house, the quality of the Darra morning sunlight into which I am squinting.

After a brief return to the pictures where I'm still asleep, having missed the end of *D.O.A.*, the scene changes to an empty dirt road under a street light. My family and I emerge from the darkness, walking home. My head is down; my feet are plodding. I'm fast asleep as we all disappear into the darkness. The stirring orchestral finale from *D.O.A.* also ends *A Photo of Me*.

Several visual elements of the film are relevant to concerns of life and death, and form a "distinct connection" between photography and cinema and the ancient forms of the non-photographic image. My interest in these themes and in the archive are focussed and framed on that moment in a backyard in Darra almost 70 years ago.

In challenging what he calls "the immaculate conception theory of photography", and showing that "the spirit of photography is much older than the photograph itself", David Hockney has made a powerful case for the influence of the camera obscura on visual art practice in Europe.[6] For centuries before the "invention" of photography was announced in 1839, artists used various forms of this "dark room" and its small hole (known since antiquity) to select what to render realistically and in a certain perspective—while choosing what to retain and what to exclude—and sometimes to combine one image with another on the surface of the work. When describing "ideas" in his *Essay Concerning Human Understanding* (1690), the philosopher John Locke also makes a remarkably accurate prediction about the future and photography.

> Would the pictures coming into such a dark room but stay there, and lie so orderly as to be found upon occasion, it would very much resemble the understanding of a man, in reference to all objects of sight, and the ideas of them.[7]

The camera obscura produced a fugitive "live" image, a projection that moved with all the colours but impermanence of life itself. The true "record" or (almost) instantaneous copy from life—the marvel of photography that Locke said would "stay there and lie so orderly"—was finally accomplished by chemistry. The daguerreotype unveiled at the Academy in Paris in 1839 (with Nadar's 1886 subject, the enthusiastic chemist Chevreul, as its President) would soon be just one of many ways of fixing the image of light and shadow.[8]

There is only one extant photographic image of Emily Dickinson confirmed by those who knew her. The image, a small daguerreotype, was probably taken by a visiting photographer whose identity remains uncertain. It is now in the collection of Amherst College near the poet's home in Amherst, Massachusetts; several years ago I viewed it by appointment. Time is short; the daguerreotype is still in its red cloth-covered hinged case and stored inside a polystyrene box. The white-gloved attendant never leaves; there is something of the mortuary or the reliquary about the viewing. (Many daguerreotypes were images of dead and embalmed children.) In celebrating the photograph as "the mirror with a memory" in 1859, Oliver Wendell Holmes goes further: "(M)atter as a visible object is of no great use any longer.... Give us a few negatives of a thing worth seeing, taken from different points of view, and that is all we want of it. Pull it down or burn it up, if you please".[9] He may have had a different view when, a year after she took his son's photographic portrait in 1884, Clover Adams committed suicide by drinking potassium cyanide, one of her photography chemicals.[10]

As a daguerreotype, the Dickinson image itself is unique, a fixed reflection of a young woman on a mirrored plate (*this same plate*) with a light-sensitive coating, in a bright room somewhere unknown. The plate was exposed just once in the camera's dark box, perhaps in late 1847. The lens cover was removed by the photographer and then, after some seconds or minutes, replaced. Depending on the angle of view, the fixed image on the plate appears as either positive or negative. Like all daguerreotypes this effect gives the image an uncanny depth. In this mirror of memory, Emily Dickinson's face is about the size of my smallest fingernail.

In his extended meditation on a photograph of his mother as a child, Roland Barthes has written movingly on the photograph and its relation to Death. Compared to the "chimeras" of painting and discourse, the very essence of photography, its *noeme*, is "that-has-been" or "the Intractable": the fact that Barthes "can never deny that the thing has been there. There is a superimposition here, of reality and of the past".[11] Further, he acknowledges the sentimental reason for his interest in photography: "I wanted to explore it not as a question (a theme) but as a wound".[12] Without an existing negative, this small paper photo of me in Darra is as unique as the Dickinson daguerreotype.

James Agee is another writer suspicious of his own words who, in the Preamble to *Let Us Now Praise Famous Men*, celebrates the photography of his collaborator Walker Evans and its direct link to the power of the Real.

> If I could do it, I'd do no writing at all here. It would be photographs; the rest would be fragments of cloth, bits of cotton, lumps of earth, records of speech, pieces of wood and iron, phials of odours, plates of food and of excrement.... A piece of body torn out by the roots might be more to the point.[13]

To paraphrase Agee: if I could do it, I'd do no animation at all in *A Photo of Me*. It would be photographs; the rest would be movies of my life in Darra, real footage of all my memories and all the times I don't remember, in all the teeming detail of life itself. Pieces of time and space torn from the past might be more to the point.

*

My father was a boilermaker by trade; though he was highly skilled with machines and building, he would never have claimed to be an artist. But, as Barthes points out, photography is different.

> Usually the amateur is defined as an immature state of the artist: someone who cannot—or will not—achieve the mastery of a profession. But in the field of photographic practice, it is the amateur, on the contrary, who is the assumption of the professional: for it is he who stands closer to the *noeme* of Photography.[14]

Soon after completing *A Photo of Me* I was contacted after more than 60 years—coincidentally, it turned out—by a former neighbour from Darra. As a young girl she had lived with her family in a concrete brick house nearby and had often played with the Tupicoff boys. She sent me several photographs taken by her father, who was later to become a professional photographer in New Zealand. There is an image of my brothers and I in a group of children at her fifth birthday party, and two other photographs of her with my two brothers.

One of these two images was very familiar; we had always had a print of it in our family's small collection of photographs. It was taken in our backyard, with the house in the background, just a few metres from where the "top and train" image used in *A Photo of Me* was taken. The focal length and the sense of composition in all these photographs, and the inclusion of the top and train as props in the photo of me, all suggest a practiced photographer— and probably not a Kodak box camera. The two images taken in our backyard are very similar; the angle of the sun indicates the same time of day. The children's ages and clothes also suggest that they could have been taken at the same time. If so, my animated reconstruction of that sunny Darra morning is wrong in one important respect—the identity of the photographer, and hence the credit to Len Tupicoff—and perhaps in many others. My older brother Gary is the only other surviving member of my immediate family, and he doesn't remember. Without memory or other evidence it is impossible to know.

NOTES

1 Anthony, Sylvia. *The Discovery of Death in Childhood and After.* Harmondsworth: Penguin Education, 1973. 199.
2 ibid. 165.
3 ibid. 163 (italics added).
4 Barthes, Roland. *Camera Lucida.* Flamingo/Fontana: London, 1984. 92.

5 Franklin, R.W. (ed). op. cit. 390 (#901).
6 Hockney, David and Gayford, Martin. *A History of Pictures*. London: Thames & Hudson, 2016. 236.
7 ibid. 212.
8 Gernsheim, Helmut and Alison. *L.J.M. Daguerre*. New York: Dover, 1968. 100.
9 Holmes, Oliver Wendell. "The Stereoscope and the Stereograph" in *The Atlantic*. June, 1859. https://www.theatlantic.com/magazine/archive/1859/06/the-stereoscope-and-the-stereograph/303361/ Retrieved 8-5-20.
10 https://en.wikipedia.org/wiki/Marian_Hooper_Adams Retrieved 8-5-20.
11 Barthes, Roland. *Camera Lucida*. op. cit. 76–77.
12 ibid. 21.
13 Agee, James and Walker Evans. op. cit. 13.
14 Barthes, Roland. *Camera Lucida*. op. cit. 98–99. (italics in original).

CHAPTER **12**

Still Alive (2018)

Well my God's not dead, he's still alive.

TRAD. ARR. THE SLAUGHTERMEN (1985)

In the world of the animated film the animator is often seen as a
God controlling all time and space, or at least "in the classic mode
of the author as animator miming the Great Animator—God".[1]
But in reality, in our shared world of human life, this animator is
as helpless as everyone else. He knows, since he both discovered
and inflicted death in his childhood—and made films about it—
that he too must die.

In 2015 I had a serious acute illness. It did not trigger hallucinations or a religious conversion or other life-changing results
of a near-death experience. Much more important was The
Slaughtermen's respectful but ironic rock version of the traditional gospel song "God's Not Dead", recorded "live" in 1985,
which I had admired since hearing it then. This was an opportunity to revisit the tradition of the skeleton and the dance of death,
and my own film *Dance of Death* after 35 years, but with me as
the performer miming the voice of Ian Stephen and with my own
movements via rotoscope. I was cheap and available and "still

alive". Like my first film *Please Don't Bury Me, Still Alive* is based firmly on an existing song but, unlike a commercial music video, is adapted to serve my narrative. And also unlike a music video there was no budget, so I was grateful for the band's permission to use their original recording.

As will become clear, this recording of "God's Not Dead" reaches down across the years to control much of the film. With appropriate diffidence I can also claim the "almost God-like omnipotence" of the auteur described by Paul Wells. As a film-maker (reluctantly now, by economic necessity) I "operate almost entirely alone. Arguably, animation may be viewed as the most auteurist of film practices in this respect, and its very process... insists upon the cohesive intervention of an authorial presence".[2]

Still Alive is structured as an allegorical presentation—an *"embodyment"* (sic)—of both human life and animation, at least in the form of drawings and photography, with which I am most familiar. The film is a hybrid of live action and animation, but in neither of the forms mentioned by Alan Cholodenko in his Introduction to *The Illusion of Life* essay collection: the lightning sketch of the earliest times and the much later digital techniques of *Who Framed Roger Rabbit?*[3] In *Still Alive* rotoscope is used to bring the "real" movement of live action into a world which is always animated, but is constantly changing. It is a "live" record-ing with a skeletal singer who later—after a mysterious sequence when the music stops—briefly becomes photographic before he resumes singing as a "live" and non-skeletal (but still hand-drawn) animated performer.

The film opens with the sounds of a forest, and in cinematic dark-ness—with its title *Still Alive* in large capitals. (As an ironic parallel to the use of the gospel song by The Slaughtermen, and in the spirit of "the Great Animator—God" mentioned earlier, some Biblical lines suggest themselves here in italics: *"In the beginning was the Word, and the Word was with God, and the Word was God".*[4]) Via a bouncing ball Genesis and a rock beat, the simple stick figure of a skeleton emerges. (*"He was in the beginning with God".*)

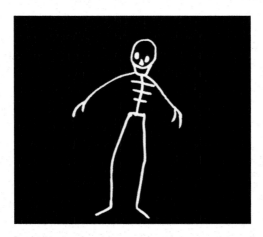

At first the Émile Cohl-esque figure is rendered—awkwardly, almost shyly—as white lines on black. ("*All things were made through Him, and without Him nothing was made that was made*".) But soon he sways to the music more confidently and becomes a clothed silhouette. ("*In Him was life, and the life was the light of men*".) Now the stage lights reveal a more realistic skeleton, the familiar figure of Don Death in his tuxedo and red bow tie—and the lively, colourful, applauding crowd from *Dance of Death*. Right on cue we are back with Don as he starts to sing. In the beginning is the word "God":

Well my God's not dead
He's still alive.
God's not dead
He's still alive.
God's not dead
He's still alive.
I can feel him in my hands
Feel him in my feet
Feel him all over me.

This song is perhaps the "old favourite" that the skeletal Don Death is about to sing in *Dance of Death* when he cues his unseen band leader: "Right now I'd like to do an old favourite of mine. Hope you like it. Ray? Thank you!". (Instead, his young viewer Sally Roberts changes channels to search for more violence and we never hear the song.) In *Still Alive* there is no dynamic "little Sally" to wield the remote control and deliver those edits to push the narrative along. But at the first opportunity, in a musical break between chorus and verse, we are given a montage of the most violent scenes from *Dance of Death*. Thirty-five years later, the studio audience still laps it up.

After a verse of sung performance and a cut to the cheering crowd, Don returns to sing another chorus. This time he moves as before, but has changed again. Though still rendered in the same graphic way, with simplified bony hands and jaw, he is noticeably "leaner", with anatomically correct proportions, and moves very naturally. He is still a drawn and clothed human skeleton, with nothing photographic, yet he has the poise and timing of a "live" performer; at one point he almost loses his balance. Don shows no extreme exaggeration of pose or foreshortening—nothing that a camera lens cannot deliver—and no sign of caricature, "squash and stretch" or anything else from the animator's repertoire. None of this is surprising, of course, since the drawings of the skeleton and his clothes were adapted by me, drawn from my own (recorded) movements while I mimed the words to playback—as Leverne McDonnell mimed the original radio voice of Kathy Easdale to playback for later rotoscoping in *His Mother's Voice*. Here, the voice of Ian Stephen from 1985 controls my mouth, as the music controls my movements. To this extent at least my "God-like" powers as an animator are shared with the ghosts of musicians past.

At this point, however, the God of this little world intervenes; he's certainly not dead. The music pauses for a narrative interlude not included in the original song—just as it does when John dies early in *Please Don't Bury Me*—and the audience disappears. Retaining its anatomically accurate proportions, and still dressed in a tuxedo and bow tie, the skeleton reverts to the white chalk outline and blackboard darkness of the earliest cartoons.

Hearing the distant sounds of trains and war, he can only peer into the infinite gloom. Soon, however, a door opens; a wedge of light illuminates the figure, and the rock music floods in. Now the door closes again; the skeleton is back in darkness. But now he is not alone; he follows the footfalls as they move around him in the darkness. An overhead light switches on above him, with a vast cheering crowd somewhere out there,

outside the cone of light. *"And the light shines in the darkness, and the darkness did not comprehend it."*

Then the light switches off. Silence and darkness again. The footfalls move towards the door, which opens with the music as before. Its light reveals that the head of the figure is now a photograph of the much younger Dennis Tupicoff who made *Dance of Death* in 1983. Now another photograph, and another. As a jerky series of stop-motion photographs I turn: "still alive" but growing older with each rotation.

The unseen God is still there, "still alive", still invisible and controlling everything: the door, the light, the crowd, the music, my body and face, my rapidly advancing age. Now the door begins to close again; the Great Animator is about to leave me to a world of darkness and silence. Alarmed, I rush towards the door, bursting through at the last moment/frame.

Now I am a drawing once more—no more photographs— and out in the light, but now as the older Dennis, not the skeletal Don Death. Once again I'm performing for the *Dance of Death* studio audience as energetically as before:

Well my God's not dead
He's still alive.
God's not dead
He's still alive.
God's not dead
He's still alive.
I can feel him in my hands
Feel him in my feet
Feel him all over me.

"He's still alive! He's still alive!" The words "STILL ALIVE" appear behind me in the huge flashing light-bulb capitals of Elvis Presley's 1968 comeback TV special.

As he chants "He's still alive! He's still alive!" the tuxedo drawing of Dennis gradually becomes simpler, more cartoon, though he is evidently unaware of his transformation by that unseen hand.

Still belting out the song, the figure changes rapidly into simpler forms of cartoon and lip sync, until it resembles one of the crowd. They are still there, still applauding in their endless eight-frame cycle.

Finally, the singer is a stick figure who has lost both individual identity and the power of speech; its mouth is one line, shut tight. (The singing voice continues; the performer has been miming all along. But the cartoon crowd doesn't care.) As the music winds down, the stick figure loses its rhythm, then staggers and falls to its knees. Soon it is reduced to a bouncing ball, the most basic of animated forms. One last bounce takes it up, away, and out of the empty black frame, as the ironic title-in-lights "STILL ALIVE" returns. The ball returns too, of course—it's an animated bouncing ball after all—but this time it does not "squash and stretch". It splats into the ground, to darkness and silence, taking the music and the Elvis-style stage graphic "STILL ALIVE" with it into oblivion. Only the forest sounds remain for the credits, as with the title earlier.

Whatever its claims to being "the illusion of life", animation is also the *"embodyment"* of death's spectral reality. Of course, it is the *illusion* of life, but one steeped in both irony and humour—like the hitman known as The Magician because people around him keep disappearing. Or ourselves as living gods in the cinema: the audience as Szymborska's "helpless gods" who see those dates of birth and death at the end of *Chainsaw*, and read "The Letters of the Dead" while we still have time.

> We read the letters of the dead like helpless gods,
> but gods, nonetheless, since we know the dates that follow...
> The dead sit before us comically, as if on buttered bread,
> or frantically pursue the hats blown from their heads.
> Their bad taste, Napoleon, steam, electricity,
> their fatal remedies for curable diseases,
> their foolish apocalypse according to St John...[5]

Caravaggio's *The Beheading of St John the Baptist* (1608) is one of many paintings that he probably made by drawing from a projected image.

> Caravaggio posed each model—like an actor in a play—and painted them more or less precisely as he saw them. We can tell that by looking closely at his paintings. To a modern eye, the results look photographic or cinematic—in other words, like pictures made with a camera, which they may well have been.[6]

The camera obscura and its place in the development of photography—the chemical fixing of a fugitive image—are dealt with elsewhere. But the use of lenses and different systems of viewing and projection found another application as one technique of achieving the "illusion of life" in animation through the use of reality itself. The rotoscope technique records with a camera both images and movement from life, but then interprets them more or less creatively, and manipulates them both in space—as artists like Caravaggio used the camera obscura for centuries—and, as cinema, in time.

Though very widespread, the use by artists of cameras under various names (camera obscura/lucida/ottica) was often hidden—allegations of easy and soulless drawing and even "cheating" were common—and its use in particular works remains contested by historians today. In the 18th century an artist like Joshua Reynolds, President of the Royal Academy, could comment sourly in print: "If we suppose a view of nature represented with all the truth of the camera obscura, and the same scene represented by a great artist, how little and mean will the one appear in comparison of the other".[7] Yet Horace Walpole tells us that both Reynolds and his Academy successor Benjamin West owned and used such a camera themselves. "Reynolds and West are gone mad with it".[8] Throughout their work on the subject, Hockney and Gayford (and Hockney in his earlier book *Secret Knowledge*[9]) insist on the individual's skills and interpretative insights as central to the artistic achievement; neither the drawing nor the painting make themselves.

Photography, of course, changed everything. The fixed permanent image was there as the present-become-past and could not be denied. Still, when Muybridge in 1878–1879 presented his series of motion studies as a series of discrete images of the horse in motion, he was met with scepticism. He had to display them as silhouettes traced by hand from the photographic images, and with their motion restored using the device called the zoopraxiscope, before viewers were convinced: "The irony perhaps—that speaks more to the birth of animation than to live cinema—is the fact that Muybridge's zoopraxiscope images were not made from photographic images but of drawings made of each photographic image—a technique now known as rotoscoping".[10]

The different paths of live action and animation are demonstrated by several very different events in 1 year: 1915. In Italy Pirandello first published his novel *Si Gira!* (*Shoot!*) in which the poor cinematograph operator Serafino Gubbio must crank the handle of his machine mechanically, as if he is a machine, whatever horrors are being recorded.[11] On 7 May 1915 the RMS

Lusitania was sunk by a torpedo in the Atlantic, an event which was to inspire McCay's *The Sinking of the Lusitania*. With that powerful animated documentary McCay demonstrated what could be achieved in animation without rotoscoping but with remarkable skill, and just how long it took to do so. The film's usefulness as propaganda was diminished by its release in 1918, near the end of the war.

And in the USA, on 6 December 1915, Max Fleischer filed his patent for the rotoscope, writing: "An object of my invention is to provide a method by which improved cartoon films may be produced, depicting the figures or other objects in a life-like manner, characteristic of the regular animated photo pictures".[12] The Fleischer studio, though happy to embrace the rotoscope, initially publicized it as a new "mystery process of lifelike action" and a "dark secret" to achieve "astounding perfection in animation".[13] Once the process was finally revealed, however, the studio acknowledged and celebrated the ghost of reality moving in many of its drawn characters, from Koko the clown to the animated form of the black entertainer Cab Calloway.

The Disney studio took a very different view. "Disney worked very hard to suppress the viewer's awareness of rotoscopic co-presence, " not only in the publicity for its *Snow White and the Seven Dwarfs* (1937) but in the animation itself.[14] As leading practitioners at the studio, Frank Thomas and Ollie Johnston portray the use of live action reference stills ("photostats") as a useful and even necessary stage in the evolution of the Disney "illusion of life".

> These were the precious elements of life revealed by the camera. But whenever we stayed too close to the photostats... the figure lost the illusion of life... it was impossible to become emotionally involved with this eerie, shadowy creature who was never a real inhabitant of our fantasy world.[15]

Under Walt's watchful eye, and despite increasingly "shooting film for specific scenes or special actions", the Disney animators claim they learnt in the 1930s to use rotoscope for reference only. "We had made the big break from rotoscope."[16] At the same time, as Esther Leslie points out, the studio's features moved steadily away from the wild world of cartoons and towards an animated imitation of cinematic realty: "The reinstitution of physical laws was most evident in the animators' dilemma when designing a scene that showed Snow White falling. They worried about the height of the drop and whether it could lead to her death".[17] In the complicated world of the feature film, and with the influence of live action, there was more than one way for hybridity to express itself in animation.

Despite the commonly expressed view that it is mere tracing and a crutch for less capable animators, the use of rotoscope has persisted down the years. In the work of Ralph Bakshi it has often been used in hybrid films with various styles of drawn animation.[18] The interpolation technique of Bob Sabiston and his Rotoshop software was used in the Richard Linklater features *Waking Life* (2001) and *A Scanner Darkly* (2006) and in various Sabiston shorts. While happy to acknowledge the obvious—that Rotoshop uses digital video as its basis—Sabiston is very keen to assure us that it does not use filters or other automation, and that it requires the skills of many human artists. When asked if *A Scanner Darkly* can be fairly described as an animated film, he answers:

> Of course…. I think a lot of people get hung up on the whether or not it is 'cheating' or 'fair' to use rotoscoping…. I'm not sure that *Waking Life* or *A Scanner Darkly* would be very good if they were traditionally animated. They need to be in that halfway point to reality. [19]

Bazin returns to haunt one of the most interesting scenes in *Waking Life*: a rather one-sided discussion seen and heard by the film's drifting protagonist. One character (played by the filmmaker Caveh Zahedi) is holding forth on film theory:

So for Bazin, what the ontology of film has to do with—
which is also what photography has an ontology of,
except that it has this dimension of time to it, which
adds this greater realism—and so it's about that guy at
that moment in that space. And Bazin is a Christian, so
he believes that God—he believes that reality and God
are the same, so that what film is actually capturing is
God incarnate, creating. At this very moment God is
manifesting as this.

This near-monologue is interrupted by the manifestation
of a mosquito on the face of the other character. Things end
badly for the mosquito—if it was ever there in the pro-filmic
world. (One suspects not, since it is never seen.) In his analysis
of the scene, Steve Reinke invokes both Bazin and this mosquito, going on to say: "*Waking Life* inhabits an indeterminate,
even liminal, realm in which we cannot say what is animated
and what is not."[20] With its protagonist at various times floating along, both figuratively and metaphorically, and uncertain
whether he is asleep or awake, living or dead, Linklater's film is
ideal for the use of rotoscope.

Many writers on photography and cinema have commented on
the reliance on or acceptance of the contingent and telling detail
associated with the exact moment when the image or images are
recorded.[21] These are the very details—fashions in hair, clothes or
car design for example, but also styles of lighting, design and performance—that can make any photographic image melancholy
or sentimental, quaint or even silly. As Antonioni demonstrates
in his adaptation of the Cortazar story, *Blow-Up* (1966), the detail
recorded by a camera, though unseen by the photographer, can
reveal strange and sinister surprises in the shadows or in the film
grain itself.[22] In telling a story, André Gaudreault says, the narrative
film is "necessarily compelled to give an account of some form of
reality—that is, the one that appeared in front of the camera—even
though it has been disguised in a fiction in order to be recorded".[23]

To the extent that it creates its own visual world, on the other hand, the animated film incurs no debt to reality. As in a painting, everything is determined; nothing is contingent. For that reason, and despite the inevitably changing fashions of graphic design and the techniques of their craft, animated films tend to date less quickly than their live action counterparts. Equally, one is unlikely to find a murder victim in the background of an animated film, as the photographer does in his photograph in *Blow-Up*. On the other hand, as Doane says in her discussion of "execution" films in the early "cinema of attractions": "Death would seem to mark the insistence and intractability of the real in representation".[24] Animation too has much in common with Death, but only as something which has never lived. Whatever its claim to being "the illusion of life", animation is marked by an absence of contingency. It is something created *in* time but moving *outside* it, a form that we might also call "the illusion of death".

In Gaudreault's terms the rotoscope technique provides an infinitely variable "disguise" by which animation can be given "some form of reality", a reality that (to paraphrase him) once appeared in front of a camera. From Fleischer's Koko the clown to the more recent "motion capture" technique used in animated films like *The Polar Express* (Zemeckis, 2004), the principle is the same: to deploy physical movement recorded in real time in another form, giving "reality" or "life" to the animation of characters and objects that exist only as drawings or computer models.

As it developed, this animation could be seen as a continuum between "the illusion of life" and life itself. Unfortunately, as the animation approaches cinematographic reality, it makes a promise—the presentation of life itself—which it usually cannot deliver. At this point the animation enters the "uncanny valley" where the viewer's emotional response falls away.[25] This was never a problem for Koko the clown. However strangely life-like in its movements, Koko was—like the characters in *Waking Life*— clearly a graphic substitute. In *The Polar Express*, however, many viewers feel uneasy about the animated character who looks and sounds *like* Tom Hanks but is pretending, "creepily", to *be* him. As the film's director, however, Robert Zemeckis is adamant that "this isn't an animated film; it's digitally rendered. The acting is all acting, the directing is all directing".[26] His attitude is characteristic of the questions of identity that have haunted this hybrid technique and its descendants from the start.

The producers of animated films can be equally trenchant in defence of their technical and aesthetic purity, and to forestall any suspicion of contamination by live action. The makers of *Waltz With Bashir* (Folman, 2008) have strongly rejected any association with rotoscope techniques—for example when presenting the film at the Annecy festival in 2008. The film uses Flash software to animate with a digital cut-out technique, but also with a great deal of photographic reference material, both still and moving. Despite the various filmic approaches used, David Polonsky's stylized but powerfully "realistic" graphic novel design is employed throughout, until the shocking final scenes of a real massacre recorded as news footage.

> Through the film's aesthetic consistency, dreams and memories are given equal epistemological weight to the present-day interviews. Hallucinations and, perhaps incorrect, recollections of the past are implied as significant as the delivery of verbal recollection. Both are evidence that can be used to unearth Folman's buried memories.[27]

In the end credits for Pixar's *Ratatouille* (Bird, 2007) is this critical disclaimer: "Our Quality Assurance Guarantee: 100% genuine ANIMATION! No motion capture or other performance shortcuts were used in the production of this film".[28]

In my earlier films I usually employed rotoscope in relatively realistic (if occasionally dreamlike) situations. In *Still Alive*, however, there is no pretence at reality. The story involves one character, starting as a chalk-line graffiti skeleton, who undergoes metamorphoses both gradual and sudden, perhaps at the hands of an invisible Someone/God. The presence of this antagonist—if it is an antagonist—is signalled by opening and closing doors, and the footfalls we hear in the darkness. There are no changes in time and place except for cutaways to the cartoon TV-show world of *Dance of Death*. This relationship is never explained, but by implication is one between an enthusiastic entertainer (first skeletal and then not) and a cartoon audience being entertained just as enthusiastically. Photographic images are used only briefly as components in a sequence that remains rotoscoped as animation. The film never looks like live action; it has no incidental or contingent action, and no backgrounds.

Yet most of the animation is based firmly on a real (rotoscoped) performance, just as it uses a "live" recording by The Slaughtermen of the song "God's Not Dead". The live action material, spectrally present but invisible, acts as a framework or armature upon which the animated drawings can be made in various degrees of illustrative realism as required by the story. The live action frames can also be ignored by the animator, when only simple drawings such as stick figures and bouncing balls are required. These are drawn freehand, as they might have been in 1900, and rapidly break free of the music. In all the worlds of animation, then and now, the animator remains the God of each one—and still alive.

*

My next animated film has no use for rotoscope or live action; it is animated with simple graphics, and with no reference to photographic reality. Once again I use my own voice to tell my own story in the first person. Once again I disappear; life ends in my death. But this time it takes place in a Queensland wheat field— and a river, and a desert—and in my adolescent past. There is no fiction or symbolism; this is a life experience—a documentary— and stranger than fiction.

NOTES

1 Cholodenko, Alan (ed). op. cit. 24.
2 Wells, Paul. op. cit. 73.
3 Cholodenko, Alan (ed). op. cit. 22–23.
4 Bible: John 1 (New King James Version).
5 Szymborska, Wislawa. op. cit. 71.
6 Martin Gayford in: Hockney, David and Gayford, Martin. op. cit. 172.
7 Hockney, David & Gayford, Martin. op. cit. 222.
8 ibid. 223.
9 Hockney, David. *Secret Knowledge*. London: Thames & Hudson, 2006.
10 Clark, David. "The Discrete Charm of the Digital Image" in: Gehman, Chris and Steve Reinke (eds). op. cit. 147.
11 Pirandello, Luigi. *op. cit.*
12 quoted in: Bouldin, Joanna. "Cadaver of the Real: Animation, Rotoscoping and the Politics of the Body": *Animation Journal* – Vol. 12, 2004. 11.
13 ibid. 17.
14 ibid. 17.
15 Thomas, Frank and Ollie Johnston. Disney Animation: The Illusion of Life. New York: Abbeville Press, 1981. 323.
16 ibid. 323.
17 Leslie, Esther. *Hollywood Flatlands: Animation, Critical Theory and the Avant-garde*. London: Verso, 2002. 149.
18 Gibson, Jon M. and Chris McDonnell. *Unfiltered: The Complete Ralph Bakshi*. New York: Rizzoli, 2008.
19 Kriger, Judith. op. cit. 28–29.
20 Reinke, Steve. "The World is a Cartoon: Stray notes on Animation" in: Gehmann, Chris and Steve Reinke (eds). op. cit. 22–23.
21 Doane, Mary Ann. *The Emergence of Cinematic Time*. Cambridge, MA: Harvard University Press, 2002. 142–143.
22 Cortazar, Julio. in: *The End of the Game and Other Stories*. New York: Harper Colophon, 1978. 114–131.
23 in Doane. op. cit. 143.
24 ibid. 145.
25 Torre, Dan. *Animation – Process, Cognition and Actuality*. op. cit. 152–154.

26 Zemeckis, Robert., interviewed by Anwar Brett http://www.bbc. co.uk/films/2004/12/01/robert_zemeckis_the_polar_express_ interview.shtml retrieved 14-5-20.

27 Honess Roe, Annabelle. *Animated Documentary.* op. cit. 163.

28 Kriger, Judith. op. cit. 19.

CHAPTER 13

The River (2020)

"In the sky before me I saw two rivers, streaming into one".

At a festival in Berkeley in 2020 the US film maker Joan C. Gratz asked me to come up with a "one-minute memoir" as part of an anthology of animated films with the same brief. She would provide a modest budget, but the content and style of the film were completely up to me. Other than that it should be a 1-minute animated memoir, Joan didn't want to know anything else: "Surprise me".

Exactly 1 minute long, *The River* (2020) is a memory from 1968 brought to life in animated form, with a narration script written and voiced by me. The first and third sections of the film, in black and white, show me as a simple silhouette on a tractor in a vast field of wheat.

The middle part of the narration script—the 40 seconds in *italics* below—is what I saw before me during the experience.

> It was 1968. I was seventeen. I was out west on a tractor, ripping up the wheat stubble. *In the sky before me I saw two rivers, streaming into one. I was in a great shoal of beings, as the river swept us along. Above me I saw the river bank like hair, waving, calling to me. Only now did I hear the wind. The desert wind.* Suddenly I was back on the tractor. I was seventeen years old. With a lot more ground to cover that day.

Suddenly, and in colour, two rivers in the sky come together as dual waterfalls: a confluence that becomes a river full of shining fish/beings.

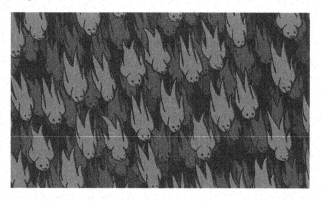

I know they are people and—though they are indistinguishable—I know which one I am amongst them. Looking up and outward to the world beyond the river, I see a veil of sand being blown off the river bank. I am drawn to it, and leave the river. On the bank, as the wind dries my skin I lose my colours from the river. I try to walk, but the wind is too strong. Now the wind-blown sand starts to tear at my skin. I grow thinner as my body is worn away. Soon I disappear in a blast of screaming wind and sand.

Between its bookends—the tractor dragging the harrow through the stubble—the narrative structure of the story is very simple: beginning, middle, and end. The experience is told and shown "as it happened", without any reflection on its possible meaning: the obvious symbolism, for instance, of the Journey from conception/birth through life to death. I want to show, as accurately as I can after more than 50 years, and within the tight limits of screen time and budget, what I saw while driving the tractor that day in 1968. In showing myself as the protagonist and using animation I deliberately choose a generalized, rather anonymous figure among many others, since that's what I remember.

The broad details—the two rivers, the screen direction of movement, my subjective point of view of the bank from beneath the water, how my body was worn away in the wind—have always been clear in my memory and needed no invention. I remember that the numberless underwater beings looked something like this and were so similar. I remember "knowing" that the "featured" figure was me and yet looked like the others, not a 17-year-old student with glasses and pimples and standing 6'10". The film could have been re-enacted as a drama and in live action, with an actor and expensive visual effects, but it would still be an approximation, an illustration of what I saw. And it would lose the simplicity and teeming anonymity of the underwater scene, followed by my short life and quick death alone on the river bank.

The Stoic philosopher Marcus Aurelius (AD 121–180) was happy to view the dead and their insignificance as providing a lesson for us, the living.

> Of the life of man the duration is but a point, its substance streaming away.... All things of the body are as a river, and the things of the soul as a dream and a vapour; and life is a warfare and a pilgrim's sojourn, and fame after death is only forgetfulness. [1]

At the age of 17, I was not yet ready to embrace oblivion with the enthusiasm of the Stoics. I had just finished my first year of university, and was away from home for the first time, having placed an advertisement for work in the *Queensland Country Life*. Unknown to me then, Hildegard of Bingen (AD 1098–1179) who did not believe in the actual reality of the Virtues she saw in her visions, said: "nevertheless in the vision they move like living beings", and were "signifying". What I had seen, both extraordinary and terrifying, was—or could be—"signifying" to me as a human being, as Hidegard's visions were to her.[2] But what did it signify to me in 1968?

During the experience it seemed to tell a complete story, to draw an arc from creation to dissolution, with a conscious decision by me to leave the river for the attractions of the river bank. Of course, it ended badly; the same elements that were so attractive visually—the wind and the sand—destroyed me.

What could this be but my life so far, and my future? On reflection perhaps it was a metaphor, a cinematic representation of my fears of leaving my family for adulthood and independence. Later I reasoned that it could have been a daydream rather than a psychotic episode. I was currently reading Patrick White's *The Tree of Man*, a powerful and poetic novel about the lives of Stan and Amy Parker and their children Ray and Thelma, an Australian country family remarkably like the Allpass family then employing me on their property "Paloma", near Glenmorgan.[3]

Or perhaps it was just an extended and particularly dramatic "train of thought". But I have waited in vain and with apprehension for another ride on that or any similar train. My earlier dramatic encounter with a train, as a child in Darra sitting under the

rails as it passed over me, was thrilling but only slightly dangerous; it was normal adventurous play. "Poetic imagination, even in
mystical experience, is… continually hovering between fancy and
conviction, play and seriousness".[4] Throughout his life William
Blake had these visions that appeared in his work: "hallucinatory
images that… are not memories, or afterimages, or daydreams,
but real sensory perceptions".[5] A London sunrise was to Blake not
a sign of planetary movement or the end of night. "When the Sun
rises do you not see a round Disk of fire somewhat like a Guinea O
no no I see an Innumerable company of the Heavenly host crying
Holy Holy Holy is the Lord God almighty".[6]

Without the comforts of religion, or much knowledge of anything metaphysical, I had to explain what I had seen to myself as
best I could. (It was too strange a tale to share with my family or my
rationalist and sceptic friends.) As well as Freud and Jung, the advice
of Mircea Eliade would have been useful to me after being on that
tractor in 1968: "Individuals who no longer have any religious experience properly speaking, reveal in their behaviour a whole camou-
flaged mythology, and fragments of a forgotten or degraded religion.
(Their) religion has become unconscious".[7] Perhaps my mind was
just a jumble of belief fragments, lost and looking for a home in some
(any) narrative of sufficiently satisfying dramatic shape.

Or was I mad? The Allpass family and others at country cricket
matches and play readings seemed to think not. And if it was a
hallucination, could I see it as "just like a movie", as I did when I
saw the priest shoot and then bash to death the dog in Darra years
before? But that dog was really dead—I had seen its brains on the
grass—and my break with religion was made permanent at that
moment. Though it later became a scene in *The Darra Dogs*, that
killing was no movie. It certainly was not fictional live action cinema, what Barthes calls the "domestication of Photography", and
thus shielded from madness. "A film can be mad by artifice, can
present the cultural signs of madness, it is never mad by nature (by
iconic status); it is always the very opposite of a hallucination; it is
simply an illusion; its vision is oneiric, not ecmnesic".[8] This last word

leaves open the madness of nature, of hallucination on that tractor, rather than "simply (the) illusion" of a dream. "Ecmnesic" is defined in McClain's helpful *Camera Lucida* glossary as an "adjective designating a delirium during the course of which the patient imagines himself to be returned to a period preceding his existence".[9] This is the source of *The River*, and why it needed to be animated.

Though it looks like a fantasy, *The River* is a 1 minute *memoir*, a non-fiction film with my own voice-over. But is it, as a memoir might claim to be, a *documentary*? As a subjective experience of wholly mental imagery, there is no "visible evidence" or archival material. There are no independent witnesses, and no documentation of physical reality at all, except for my (very vivid and disturbing) memory of an event that took place more than 50 years ago. I wrote letters to family and friends from the property in 1968, but did not mention this experience. As writer, director and sole eyewitness, and with only a minute available for this very short film, I try to keep my narrative factual and straightforward, without any reflections or interpretations of what the experience could have been, what it meant, or its effect on me. Though the story is very different and my voice was recorded 50 years—not several weeks—after the events described, my narrative model is Kathy Easdale's factual account in *His Mother's Voice*.

In discussing that film, Bill Nichols acknowledges the power of the metaphorical image, even if it is animated and therefore without the reality of the photographic image. "Animated images tap the full resources of the creative imagination and, in documentaries, become yoked to specific situations and events and, often, to the voices of actual people".[10] The voice of Kathy Easdale was used with her informed permission, but without any other direct input from her. In that sense *His Mother's Voice* is another type of hybrid: a documentary account by one person (often an eyewitness) with filmic interpretation and images by another (the film maker). This of course is the usual mode for telling an eye-witness story in documentary. Even in animated documentaries which present subjective experience and mental states, the animation is usually made by a non-subject. *Ryan* (Chris Landreth, 2004) includes animation made decades earlier by its primary subject, Ryan Larkin. As director and fellow subject, Landreth also includes animated images of himself and his own mental state at times in the past. By doing so he acknowledges his subjectivity and its influence on the film, making it both biography and autobiography: "We don't see things as *they* are, but as *we* are".[11]

Both Nichols[12] and Honess Roe[13] discuss Jonathan Hodgson's *Feeling My Way* as a walk to work that uses animation and text with xerographed video footage "to imagine an everyday and relatable state of mind—the mental meanderings and stream of consciousness that accompany a regular and uneventful routine".[14] The presence of animated skeletons drawn over the bodies of commuters in motion indicates that "uneventful" refers only to the live action world of the commuters, not to Hodgson's amusing and arresting subjective journey to his "Parallel Universe". With its direct autobiographical narrative and voice-over by the film maker, *The River* is more typical of the many animated films made in this mode. Without any photographic material, however, its ambition is for the animated images to stand not as "the illusion of life" but as a representation of a different reality—hallucinatory and perhaps psychotic—that once briefly engulfed me.

In *Pictures and Tears*, James Elkins writes movingly of tears as *witnesses*. "They leak from our eyes and run down our cheeks. They show, without room for doubt, that *something* has happened.... I like to think of tears as travellers who have come to see us from some distant country".[15] In an earlier work Elkins similarly makes room for the "unrepresentable": images such as "dreams, evanescent entopical displays, hallucinations, and half-forgotten notions of pictures".[16] In a documentary world historically dominated by the photographic image with its presumed complete representability, whether moving or still, the vast range of animation techniques provide the tools to explore everything else. "The unrepresentable can only be experienced as something that resists presentation while also lending itself—partly and with forms held in reserve—to actual pictures".[17] These animated pictures and the sounds to accompany them can be "drawn" from the whole history of human creativity to show states of mind, emotions and experiences that are subjective and conscious but often strange. In doing so, they bear witness to another reality. Like tears, they are travellers from some distant country.

*

In 2020, soon after completing *The River*, I found an online reference to the *Diaries 1950s-2016* of Isabel Marion Allpass (1926–2018) deposited before her death with the Oxley Library, part of the State Library of Queensland in Brisbane. (As mentioned earlier, my first job after graduation in 1971 was at the Queensland State Archives, a branch of the same State Library.) Isabel and her older brother "Rod" (Roderic James Allpass 1923–2014) were the two unmarried children of Mr. & Mrs. F.J. "Eric" Allpass, of "Paloma", near Glenmorgan on the western Darling Downs. Isabel's diary from late 1968, written with a blue fountain pen when she was 42, is mostly taken up with social activities, cricket scores and—relentlessly—the weather. She makes just a few mentions of me. My arrival on November 21 is the only significant one.

> *Thursday 21st.* Slightly cooler – 102°…. We decided to make sandwiches at home and to have cakes etc. with it. Also to have cold drinks there for the young ones. The student

Dennis (?) arrived in the morning—he's about 6′10″ tall!!!
You've never seen anyone such a size! He drove up in a little
Morris. *Friday 22nd.* A sultry oppressive day and the wire-
less is alive with static but there's no rain about here.[18]

My crashing into the homestead gate when returning after work
is not mentioned in the diary (the farm vehicle had faulty brakes);
nor is my departure just before Christmas. The diary of Isabel
Allpass doesn't change anything about the experience shown
in the film. Though our relationship was convivial enough, the
experience shown in *The River* wasn't something I shared with the
Allpass family at the dinner table.

*

In its combination of technique and subject *The River* aims to
"use animation to achieve poetic goals mixed with autobiographical, diaristic, and performative models and modes".[19]
Without rotoscope, photographs, or live action, an illustrated
cartoon animation style is used to tell a strange but entirely *factual* (if subjective and bizarre) story. Conversely, a film like *Still
Alive* uses various illustrative animation styles, some based on
live action via rotoscope, to tell a *fantasy* story—drawings of a
singing skeleton and then a singing me—with no claim to historical reality but with me as a recognizable face and figure, both
drawn and photographic.

The River may claim to be both historical and hysterical. As
an image of a lived experience in 1968—of time and space going
by, both unrepeatable and unrecordable—it shares some qualities
with the eidetic images seen in the mind of the poet Shelley. Before
the invention of photography, Shelley "could throw a veil over his
eyes and find himself in a camera obscura, where all the features
of a scene were reproduced in a form more pure and perfect than
they had been originally presented to his external senses".[20] But
it is also like Blake's, both hallucinatory and real, with the mind
looking on even as it participates helplessly in the experience.

As a hybrid itself, *The River* also participated in another hybrid form. The *One Minute Memoir* anthology combined in one programme many other equally short films about which I knew nothing. They were entirely separate in subject, treatment, and animation technique but, as animated memoirs, were all dealing with the idea of animated non-fiction in their own ways.

NOTES

1 Quoted in: Dollimore, Jonathan. *Death, Desire and Loss in Western Culture*. London: Penguin, 1999. 33.
2 Quoted in: Huizinga, Johan. *Homo Ludens: A Study of the Play-Element in Culture*. Kettering, OH: Angelico Press, 2016. 141.
3 White, Patrick. op. cit.
4 Huizinga, Johan. op. cit. 141.
5 Ackroyd, Peter. *Blake*. London: Vintage, 1999. 24.
6 ibid. 317.
7 Quoted in: Anthony, Sylvia. op. cit. 250.
8 Barthes, Roland. *Camera Lucida*. op. cit. 117.
9 McClain, David. "Camera Lucida: Select Terms Defined." 4. http://www.davidmcclain.com/TERMS.pdf accessed 20-5-2020.
10 Nichols, Bill. *Introduction to Documentary*. Bloomington: Indiana University Press, 2010. 110–111.
11 Chris Landreth quoted in Honess Roe, Annabelle. *Animated Documentary*. op. cit. 132.
12 Nichols, Bill. op. cit. 164.
13 Honess Roe, Annabelle. *Animated Documentary*. op. cit. 132–135.
14 ibid. 132.
15 Elkins, James. *Pictures and Tears*. New York: Routledge, 2004. 39 (italics in original).
16 James Elkins, quoted in Honess Roe, Annabelle. *Animated Documentary*. London, New York: Palgrave Macmillan, 108.
17 ibid. 108.
18 Allpass, Isabel. *Diaries 1950s -2016*. John Oxley Library, State Library of Queensland. Identifier Reference code: 30518 (Boxes 20376 O/S, 20383 O/S).
19 Nichols, Bill. op. cit. 64.
20 Medwin, Thomas. *The Life of Percy Bysshe. Shelley*. Vol. 1. London: Thomas Cautley Newby, 1847. 124.

CHAPTER 14

The End of the Matter

Sweet Thames, run softly till I end my song,
Sweet Thames, run softly, for I speak not loud or long.
But at my back in a cold blast I hear
The rattle of the bones, and chuckle spread from ear to ear.

"THE WASTELAND"—TS ELIOT (1922)[1]

Invoking Marvell's 17th-century poem "To His Coy Mistress" for his own purposes in 1922, Eliot also draws together laughter and horror, life and death, though in a very different way. For all its claims to being "the illusion of life", animation is also a cold gust of death, a rattle of bones as its chuckle spreads from screen to audience—especially when the film maker is trying to answer that question: "Why are all your films about death?"

There is no simple answer, and certainly no programme, agenda or plan according to which these films have been made. There are many other films I have written and planned but never made. But even in those phantom films there is an undeniable pattern of references to death: the repeatedly unsuccessful firing squad; the animator who dies in the first few minutes, then argues with and defies a Death who takes various forms both fearsome and entertaining; the two skeletons who operate as comic ushers in the world of the newly dead, at the direction of Kali, the Goddess of Death. And so on…. (Cue: more chuckles and rattling bones.) At its silliest and most absurd, as in its most serious narratives, the last laugh in animation is on the living. (It is, after all, the *illusion* of life.) And since death is the absence of life, we keep disappearing, becoming absent. We—the living animators whose work appears on screen as that animated illusion—become Them, the dead.

I'm clearly alive to write these words, but many people who contributed to these ten films since 1976 are dead. Among them are the great American bluegrass musicians Vassar Clements and Mike Auldridge whose work from the 1970s is heard throughout *Chainsaw*;[2] my friend Craig Carter who made the soundtracks for many of the later films; and another friend, the actor Leverne McDonnell who plays Kathy Easdale in *His Mother's Voice*.

Any screening of that film is a reminder of the hour or so Leverne spent in front of my video camera, not only inhabiting the role of a grieving mother but also knowing every word and pause of the real Kathy Easdale's voice, miming each tiny detail of her breath and lips. Later drawn in charcoal as animation, Leverne is a powerful presence in the film, bringing the original audio interview to life with the particular and deliberate trace of life that rotoscope animation can bring to the moving image. Before Leverne's own life ended in 2013, she co-produced a live action documentary advocating the cause of voluntary euthanasia, using her life and her own fatal disease as central elements.[3]

Though I had followed his career off and on since I heard his song "Please Don't Bury Me" that day in Christchurch in 1974, I met the American singer/songwriter John Prine only once. It was after an outdoor concert at the Hanging Rock racetrack in country Victoria, under the 6-million-year-old rock where the schoolgirls and their teacher disappeared forever in Joan Lindsay's novel (1967)[4] and Peter Weir's feature adaptation (1975).[5] After Prine's solo performance that cold and windy afternoon in about 1989, our daughter Zelda and I joined an orderly queue of fans outside the little wooden jockeys' shed. She was then 4 years old, not long before she asked for a dog and precipitated *The Darra Dogs*. John shook our hands—Zelda was confident and happy to introduce herself—and we made small talk for a short time; I noticed John was smoking a small dark cigarillo. I may have mentioned that I had made a cartoon of his song; certainly I sent a tape to his office in Nashville soon after. Aware of the people waiting behind us outside the jockeys' room, we said our goodbyes and left.

I saw John Prine play only once more: on his 2019 Australian tour with his band and his latest Grammy-nominated album *The Tree of Forgiveness*.[6] These days, aged 72, he danced and shimmied his way off-stage at the end of the show. The last track on the album, "When I Get to Heaven", once again addressed the subject of death and the afterlife—once again, like "Please Don't Bury Me" in 1973, in a humorous way.

> When I get to heaven, I'm gonna shake God's hand
> Thank him for more blessings than one man can stand
> Then I'm gonna get a guitar and start a rock-n-roll band
> Check into a swell hotel, ain't the afterlife grand?
> And then I'm gonna get a cocktail, vodka and ginger ale
> Yeah, I'm gonna smoke a cigarette that's nine miles long
> I'm gonna kiss that pretty girl on the tilt-a-whirl
> 'Cause this old man is goin' to town.

In March 2020, after a trip to Europe, Prine was hospitalized with the Covid 19 virus. In the last 20 years, he had suffered from neck cancer and lung disease—I thought of that cigarillo—so he was very vulnerable. Soon he was on a respirator and unconscious. Meanwhile, here in Melbourne, I completed a draft of Chapter 2—on *Please Don't Bury Me*—on April 7, 2020.

After 10 days on a respirator, John Prine died later that day in Nashville, aged 73.

*

The end or absence of life—what might be called death—has clearly been a pre-occupation in these ten films, as it is in the discussion of both photography and animation. Some films are concerned with the realization and continuing consciousness of our inevitable death as a uniquely human attribute; others use animation to deal with fantasy and reality in different combinations of humour and horror.

But these animated films about death are also about life: in their origins—in my imagination but also in newspaper stories, radio programmes, government policies, and a question from a young daughter—and in their concerns with humour, memory, emotional experience, and storytelling itself. As writer/director the films were made as part of my life from 1975 to 2020, at the mercy of time, circumstance, and money. The chronology below demonstrates that mine has not been a continuous life of animation or even film-making. Between the ten films are gaps and overlaps that indicate other activities and in turn other concerns: television commercials and other sponsored work, children's television, live-action documentaries, writing, films planned but never produced, teaching, parenting, living. It's only fitting that the discussion of each film has included a particular focus on life as well as death.

Please Don't Bury Me (1975–76): the importance of craft in animation as part of a working life.

Dance of Death (1981–83): television violence as entertainment, and as part of life.

The Darra Dogs (1990–93): drawings bring my childhood memories and dogs to life.

His Mother's Voice (1995–97): a tragic life event told from two points of view, both with the same voice of the grieving mother.

The Heat, The Humidity (1998–99): obsession drives the lives of both a cartoon robber and a famous criminal.

Into the Dark (2000–01): childhood memories and the end of life in the mind of one person.

Chainsaw (1996–2007): life as a web of intersecting stories: human and animal, past and present.

A Photo of Me (2016–17): one photograph is taken from a life of other memories and dreams.

Still Alive (2017–2018): drawings and rotoscope bring me to photographic life—and back to nothing—singing "God's Not Dead".

The River (2020): a visionary life experience is shown as it really happened.

There is a clear distinction between the genesis of each film in the past—in my time—and my view as I write today. However near or far, this distance has allowed me to see influences and connections, ironies, and interpretations that help to explain how and why, for all their variety and concern with life, these ten films *are* all about death.

If as humans we are locked in a fateful dance of death, it is also a dance of life. Animation has never lived, but is made by very mortal humans in their very limited time. When it plays on screen "the illusion of life" lives in its own time, the present of its animated life—which is also our time. However illusory it may be, animation has the unique ability to present the two dances as one, moving to the music of time.

NOTES

1 in: Bloom, Harold (ed.) op. cit. 909.
2 Auldridge, Mike. *Dobro*. Takoma Records, 1972.
3 Cochrane, Fiona (dir). *All In Her Stride*. (2014) F-reel Productions.
4 Lindsay, Joan. *Picnic at Hanging Rock*. Melbourne: FW Cheshire, 1967.
5 Weir, Peter (dir). *Picnic at Hanging Rock*. (1975) McElroy & McElroy Productions.
6 Prine, John. *The Tree of Forgiveness*. Oh Boy Records, 2018.

Appendix 1: Ten Animated Films by Dennis Tupicoff 1976–2020

PLEASE DON'T BURY ME (1976) 4:33

John wakes up, slips on the floor and dies. He goes to a Hollywood Paradise, but insists that his body should be used, not buried. A cartoon adaptation of the comic song by John Prine.

director, producer, animation—Dennis Tupicoff

song—John Prine

guitar/vocal—Dave Lemon

produced with the assistance of the Experimental Film and Television Fund

DANCE OF DEATH (1983) 8:39

An animated comedy about television violence set in a world where the skeletal Don Death runs a popular variety show called

"Dance of Death". In her suburban home, young Sally Roberts chases all the excitement of death in its many forms on TV. But in the segment of his show called "This Is Your Death", Don Death has a huge surprise for the Roberts family.

writer director—Dennis Tupicoff

voices—Matthew King, Suzanne Zenz, Brenda Beddison, Peter Curtin, Beverley Dunn, Hamish Hughes

animation—Dennis Tupicoff

music—Peter Sullivan

sound designer—Brett Southwick

producer—Dennis Tupicoff

produced in association with the Australian Film Commission

THE HEAT, THE HUMIDITY (1999) 4:36

A bank robber flies into a tropical town on professional business. But all he hears is one line, over and over: "It's not the heat, it's the humidity".

First the weather frustrates him, wrecking his plans. Then it destroys him.

writer director—Dennis Tupicoff

voices—Leverne McDonnell, Hamish Hughes, Terry Doolan

animation—Dennis Tupicoff

music—Burkhard Dallwitz

sound designer—David Harrison

technical director—Paul Connor

producer—Dennis Tupicoff

in association with the Australian Film Commission, Film Victoria, SBS Independent

THE DARRA DOGS (1993) 9:58

One day my 5-year-old daughter said that she wanted to have a dog. In trying to explain to her my feelings about dogs, I realized how much the dogs of my childhood still haunted me. These memories were still so clear and strong that I drew them into animated life. These are The Darra Dogs.

writer director producer—Dennis Tupicoff

animation—Dennis Tupicoff

music—Burkhard Dallwitz

sound designer—David Harrison

produced by Dennis Tupicoff

in association with the Australian Film Commission

HIS MOTHER'S VOICE (1997) 14:25

A mother tells how she found out that her teenage son was dead. Using the original ABC radio interview, His Mother's Voice uses rotoscoped animation to present Kathy Easdale's account from two very different points of view.

director/producer—Dennis Tupicoff

cast—Leverne McDonnell, Christopher Connelly

camera—Kath Chambers, Dennis Tupicoff

art director—Margaret Eastgate

rotoscope animation (cel)—Dennis Tupicoff

rotoscope animation (charcoal)—Annette Trevitt

music—Burkhard Dallwitz

sound designer—David Harrison

produced by Dennis Tupicoff

in association with the Australian Film Commission

INTO THE DARK (2001) 6:03

As a man dies, his mind drifts back to the evenings of his childhood: shooting birds, trying to feel nothing.

writer director—Dennis Tupicoff

producers—Fiona Cochrane, Dennis Tupicoff

animation—John Skibinski, Dennis Tupicoff, Craig L. Brookes

sound—David Harrison

music—Brahms / Idil Biret (piano)

a Jungle Pictures production

in association with the Australian Film Commission, Film Victoria, SBS Independent

CHAINSAW (2007) 24:31

The dangers of chainsaws, of bucking bulls, of the Spanish bull-fight: "It is like being with your lover when her husband comes in with a gun. The bull is the woman, the husband, and the pistol—all in one. No other life can give you all that".
Romance is like a chainsaw: a very dangerous beast indeed.

writer director—Dennis Tupicoff

producers—Fiona Cochrane, Dennis Tupicoff

visual effects supervisor: David Tait

animation—John Skibinski

rotoscope animation—Stuart Murray, John Skibinski, Rosi Osman, Alan Bell, Dennis Tupicoff

compositor/CGI—David Tait

sound designer—Craig Carter

music—Mike Auldridge, David Herzog

original music produced by Burkhard Dallwitz

live action cast—Luke Elliot, Adam Pierzschalski, Anni Davey

voices—David Cameron, Nina Landis, Luke Elliot

cinematography—Zbigniew Friedrich

production and costume designer—Adele Flere

editors—Zbigniew Friedrich, David Tait

a Jungle Pictures production

in association with the Australian Film Commission, Film Victoria, SBS Independent

A PHOTO OF ME (2017) 10:49

I'm a baby in a 1950s backyard, facing a box camera. I'm a sleepy child at the Darra "pictures", waking up to a film noir, watching a doomed man. My mind flickers from past to present, in memories and dreams. The man dies. Click! The photo is taken. I walk home from the "pictures", fast asleep.

writer director animator—Dennis Tupicoff

cast: Robert Serong, Ruben Ray, Zelda Tupicoff, Jessie Roper, Paris Scott, Dennis Tupicoff

camera, post production—David Tait

photos by Len Tupicoff (1951/2)

archival film—*D.O.A.* (1950) public domain

producer—Dennis Tupicoff

associate producer—Fiona Cochrane

a Jungle Pictures production

STILL ALIVE (2018) 5:54

An ironic and irreverent view of animation—its history and Animator-as-Creator "theology"—using the traditional gospel song "God's Not Dead".

writer director animator—Dennis Tupicoff

music—The Slaughtermen

camera edit post-production—David Tait

sound design—Emma Bortignon

mix—Paul Pirola

producer—Dennis Tupicoff

associate producer—Fiona Cochrane

a Jungle Pictures production

THE RIVER (2020) 1:07

It was 1968. I was 17. I was out west on a tractor, ripping up the wheat stubble. Suddenly in the sky before me I saw two rivers, streaming into one. Then I was in a great shoal of beings, as the river swept us along. Above me I saw the river bank like hair, waving, calling to me. Then I was on the bank. Only now did I hear the wind: the desert wind, howling, wearing me away.

writer director animator—Dennis Tupicoff

visual effects supervisor: David Tait

music and sound design—Judith Gruber-Stitzer

from: THE ONE-MINUTE MEMOIR 16'30 (2020)

producer—Joan C. Gratz

a Gratzfilm Production

Appendix 2: Other Films by Dennis Tupicoff (Writer/Director/ Producer/Co-Producer)

ANIMATED FILMS

Great Queenslanders. (1975) silent. 2 minutes.
Spaghetti. (1975) silent. 30 seconds.
Jack Fig. (1977) Swinburne Film & TV School. 3 minutes.
My Big Chance. (1977) Swinburne Film & TV School. 1 minute.
Changes. (1977) Swinburne Film & TV School. 4 minutes.
Title & Credit sequence, interstitial "spots" for *STAX.* (1978/9) Generation Films.
Puffed Out. (1980) Film Victoria. 5 minutes.
Something Tells Me. (1992) segment of *Lift Off* Series 1 Episode 16, Australian Children's Television Foundation. 3 minutes.

LIVE ACTION FILMS

The Bear. (1990) Dennis Tupicoff. 30 minutes.

Taringa 4068: Our Place and Time. (2002) Jungle Pictures. 25 minutes.

Silly and Serious: William Robinson and Self Portraits. (2008) Jungle Pictures. 25 minutes.

The First Interview. (2011) Jungle Pictures. 15 minutes, 27 minutes.

Bibliography

Ackroyd, Peter. *Blake*. London: Vintage, 1999.

Adair, Gilbert (ed.) *Movies*. London: Penguin, 1999.

Agee, James and Walker Evans. *Let Us Now Praise Famous Men*. Boston: Houghton Mifflin, 1969.

Alison, Jane. *Meander, Spiral, Explode: Design and Pattern in Narrative*. New York: Catapult, 2020.

Allpass, Isabel. *Diaries 1950s -2016*. John Oxley Library, State Library of Queensland. Identifier Reference code: 30518 (Boxes 20376 O/S, 20383 O/S).

Anderson, Laurie. *All the Things I Lost in the Flood*. New York: Rizzoli Electa, 2018.

Anon. "Spain's Greatest Matador Lays Down His Sword". Melbourne: *The Age*: 10-5-1996. 9.

Anthony, Sylvia. *The Discovery of Death in Childhood and After*. Harmondsworth: Penguin Education, 1973.

Aries, Philippe Aries. *Images of Man and Death*. Cambridge, MA: Harvard University Press. 1985.

Aries, Philippe Aries. *The Hour of Our Death*. London: Allen Lane, 1981.

Aries, Phillipe. *Western Attitudes Toward Death from the Middle Ages to the Present*. London: Marion Boyars, 1976.

Auldridge, Mike. *Dobro*. Takoma Records, 1972.

Barthes, Roland. *Camera Lucida*. London: Flamingo/Fontana, 1984.

Barthes, Roland. *Image-Music-Text*. New York: Hill and Wang, 1977.

Barthes, Roland. *Roland Barthes*. New York: Hill and Wang, 2010.

Batchen, Geoffrey (ed). *Photography Degree Zero: Reflections on Roland Barthes's Camera Lucida*. Cambridge, MA: The MIT Press, 2011.

Batchen, Geoffrey. *Each Wild Idea: Writing Photography History*. Cambridge, MA: The MIT Press, 2002.

Bazin, Andre. *What is Cinema? Vol.1* Berkeley and Los Angeles: University of California Press, 1967.

Beckman, Karen (ed). *Animating Film Theory*. Durham: Duke University Press, 2014.

Bendazzi, Giannalberto (ed). *Alexeieff—Itinerary of a Master*. CICA, Annecy—Dreamland Paris—Cinematheque Francaise, Paris, 2001.

Bendazzi, Giannalberto. *Animation: A World History (Volume 1: Foundations—The Golden Age)*. Boca Raton, FL: CRC Press, 2016.

Bendazzi, Giannalberto. *Animation: A World History (Volume 2: The Birth of a Style—The Three Markets)*. Boca Raton, FL: CRC Press, 2016.

Bendazzi, Giannalberto. *Animation: A World History (Volume 3: Contemporary Times)*. Boca Raton, FL: CRC Press, 2016.

Bendazzi, Giannalberto. *Cartoons: One Hundred Years of Cinema Animation*. London: John Libbey, 1994.

Benjamin, Walter. *Illuminations*. New York: Schocken Books, 1969.

Bermel, Alfred. *Farce*. New York: Touchstone, 1982.

Bible: John 1 (New King James Version).

Bident, Christophe. *Maurice Blanchot: A Critical Biography*. New York: Fordham, 2020.

Bierce, Ambrose. *In the Midst of Life and Other Tales*. New York: New American Library, 1961.

Biro, Yvette. *Profane Mythology: The Savage Mind of the Cinema*. Bloomington: Indiana University Press, 1982.

Blair, Preston. *How to Animate Film Cartoons*. Tustin, CA: Walter T. Foster, 1980.

Blanchot, Maurice. *The Instant of My Death*. & Derrida, Jacques. *Demeure: Fiction and Testimony*. Stanford, CA: Stanford University Press, 2000.

Blanchot, Maurice. *The Station Hill Blanchot Reader: Fiction and Literary Essays*. Barrytown, NY: Station Hill Press, 1999.

Bloom, Harold (ed.) *The Best Poems of the English Language*. New York: Harper Collins, 2004.

Bok, Gordon. *Peter Kagan and the Wind*. Folk Legacy Records, 1971.

Bond, Anthony and Joanna Woodall. *Self Portrait: Renaissance to Contemporary*. London: National Portrait Gallery, 2005.

Boorman, John. *Money into Light: a Diary*. London: Faber & Faber, 1985.

Bordwell, David. *Narration in the Fiction Film*. London: Methuen, 1985.

Botsford, Keith. *Dominguin*. Chicago: Quadrangle Books, 1972.

Bouldin, Joanna. "Cadaver of the Real: Animation, Rotoscoping and the Politics of the Body": *Animation Journal*, Vol. 12, 2004.

Broadbent Friedman, Diane. *A Matter of Life and Death: The Brain Revealed by the Mind of Michael Powell*. Bloomington, IN: AuthorHouse, 2008.

Brodkey, Harold. *This Wild Darkness: the Story of My Death*. London: Fourth Estate, 1996.

Buchan, Suzanne (ed). *Animated Worlds*. Eastleigh: John Libbey Publishing, 2006.

Bukatman, Scott. *The Poetics of Slumberland*. Berkeley: University of California Press, 2012.

Canales, Jimena. *A Tenth of a Second*. Chicago: University of Chicago Press, 2009.

Canemaker, John. *Winsor McCay: His Life and Art*. New York: Abbeville Publishers, 1987.

Chion, Michel. *The Voice in Cinema*. New York: Columbia University Press, 1999.

Cholodenko, Alan (ed). *The Illusion of Life: Essays on Animation*. Sydney: Power Publications, 1991.

Cholodenko, Alan (ed). *The Illusion of Life 2: More Essays on Animation*. Sydney: Power Publications, 2006.

Christie, Ian (ed). *Powell, Pressburger and Others*. London: BFI, 1978.

Christie, Ian. *A Matter of Life and Death*. London: BFI, 2000.

Coleman, Peter and Les Tanner. *Cartoons of Australian History*. Melbourne: Thomas Nelson, 1978.

Combs, C. Scott. *Deathwatch: American Film, Technology and the End of Life*. New York: Columbia University Press, 2014.

Cortazar, Julio. *The End of the Game and Other Stories*. New York: Harper Colophon, 1978.

Cotte, Olivier. *Le Grand Livre des Techniques du Cinéma du'Animation*. Paris: Dunod, 2018.

Crafton, Donald. *Before Mickey: The Animated Film 1898–1928*. Boston: MIT Press, 1982.

Crafton, Donald. *Emile Cohl, Caricature, and Film*. Princeton, NJ: Princeton University Press, 1990.

Crafton, Donald. *Shadow of a Mouse*. Berkeley: University of California Press, 2012.

Crary, Jonathan. *Techniques of the Observer: On Vision and Modernity in the Nineteenth Century*. Cambridge, MA: MIT Press, 1992.

Crumb, R. and Peter Poplaski. *The R. Crumb Handbook*. London: MQP Publications, 2005.

Crumb, R. *R.Crumb's Carload of Comics*. New York: Belier Press, 1976.

Culhane, Shamus. *Animation from Script to Screen*. New York: St Martin's Griffin Press, 1990.

Dancyger, Ken and Jeff Rush. *Alternative Scriptwriting: Writing Beyond the Rules*. Boston, London: Focal Press, 1991.

Darke, Chris. *La Jetée*. London: BFI & Palgrave, 2016.

Dawson, Jonathan and Bruce Molloy. *Queensland Images in Film and Television*. St Lucia: University of Queensland Press, 1990.

Dawson, Jonathan. *Screenwriting: A Manual*. South Melbourne: Oxford University Press, 2000.

Day, Douglas. *Malcolm Lowry: A Biography*. New York: Oxford University Press, 1974.

De Blois, Marco. "Eros and Thanatos" article on CHAINSAW in: (eds.) Chris Robinson and Brittany Mumford. *40 Years of OTTAWA: Collected Essays on Award Winning Animation.* Ottawa Animation Festival, 2016.

Death (personification). https://en.wikipedia.org/wiki/Death_(personification) Retrieved 28.1.20.

Deleuze, Gilles. *Cinema 1: The Movement-Image.* Minneapolis: University of Minneapolis Press, 1986.

Deleuze, Gilles. *Cinema 2: The Time-Image.* Minneapolis: University of Minneapolis Press, 1989.

Detweiler, Robert. "The Moment of Death in Modern Fiction". University of Wisconsin Press: *Contemporary Literature*, Vol. 13(3), 269–294, Summer 1972.

Dillon, Brian. "War, Love and Weirdness: A Matter of Life and Death." *The Guardian* 4/11/2016. https://www.theguardian.com/film/2016/nov/04/war-love-and-wierdness-a-matter-of-life-and-death-70-years-on Retrieved 28.1.20.

Dinnage, Rosemary. *The Ruffian on the Stair: Reflections on Death.* London: Penguin, 1992.

Doane, Mary Ann. *The Emergence of Cinematic Time.* Cambridge, MA: Harvard University Press, 2002.

Dobson, Nichola, Annabelle Honess Roe, Amy Ratelle and Caroline Ruddell (eds). *The Animation Studies Reader.* New York, London: Bloomsbury Academic, 2020.

Dollimore, Jonathan. *Death, Desire and Loss in Western Culture.* London: Penguin, 1999.

Dostoevsky, Fyodor. "Letter to His Brother" quoted in: https://www.usrepresented.com/2014/02/02/dostoevsky/ retrieved 5-3-20.

Duttlinger, Carolin. *Kafka and Photography.* New York: Oxford University Press, 2007.

Elkins, James. *Pictures and Tears.* New York: Routledge, 2004.

Enright, D.J. (ed.) *The Oxford Book of Death.* Oxford, New York: Oxford University Press, 1983.

Estren, Mark James. *A History of Underground Comics.* San Francisco, CA: Straight Arrow Books, 1974.

Faulkner, William. *Requiem for a Nun.* Harmondsworth: Penguin, 1967.

Ferretti, Val. S. and David L. Scott. *Death in Literature.* New York: McGraw-Hill, 1977.

Fibicher, Bernhard (ed) Kunstmuseum Bern. *Six Feet Under: Autopsy of Our Relation to the Dead.* Leipzig: Kerber, 2006.

Field, Sid. *Screenplay: The Foundations of Screenwriting.* New York: Dell Publishing, 1979.

Fitzsimons, Trish, Pat Laughren and Dugald Williamson. *Australian Documentary: History. Practices and Genres.* New York: Cambridge University Press, 2011.

Frank, Hannah. (Daniel Morgan: ed). *Frame by Frame: A Materialist Aesthetics of Animated Cartoons.* Oakland, CA: University of California Press, 2020.

Franklin, R.W. (ed). *The Poems of Emily Dickinson.* Cambridge, MA.: Belknap Press, 1999.

Furniss, Maureen. *Animation: The Global History.* London: Thames & Hudson, 2017.

Furniss, Maureen. *Art in Motion: Animation Aesthetics.* London: John Libbey, 1998.

Furniss, Maureen. *The Animation Bible: A Guide to Everything—from Flipbooks to Flash.* London: Lawrence King Publishing, 2008.

Gallasch, Keith. "The View from the Child". *Realtime 51,* Oct-Nov 2002 http://www.realtimearts.net/article/issue51/6875 retrieved 5-3-20.

Gardner, Ava. *Ava: My Story.* New York: Bantam Books, 1990.

Garriock, P.R. *Masters of Comic Book Art.* London: Aurum Press, 1978.

Gehman, Chris and Steve Reinke (eds). *The Sharpest Point: Animation at the End of Cinema.* Toronto: YVZ Books, 2005.

Gernsheim, Helmut and Alison. *L.J.M. Daguerre.* New York: Dover, 1968.

Gibson, Jon M. and Chris McDonnell. *Unfiltered: The Complete Ralph Bakshi.* New York: Rizzoli, 2008.

Gilliam, Terry. *Animations of Mortality.* London: Eyre Methuen, 1978.

Godfrey, Bob and Anna Jackson. *The Do-It-Yourself Animation* Book. London: BBC Publications, 1974.

Goffman, Erving. *Frame Analysis: An Essay on the Organization of Experience.* Boston: Northeastern University Press, 1986.

Grant, Barry Keith and Jeannette Sloniowski. *Documenting the Documentary.* Detroit: Wayne State University Press, 1998.

Gray, Milton. *Cartoon Animation: Introduction to a Career.* Northridge, Lion's Den, 1992.

Gunning, Tom. "The Cinema of Attraction: Early Film, Its Spectator and the Avant-Garde" in: *Wide Angle.* 8.3. Baltimore: Johns Hopkins University Press, 1986.

Halas, John and Bob Privett. *How to Cartoon for Amateur Films.* London and New York: Focal Press, 1958. (3rd edition).

Halas, John and Roger Manvell. *Art in Movement.* London: Studio Vista, 1970.

Halas, John and Roger Manvell. *The Technique of Film Animation.* London and New York: Focal Press, 1971 (3rd ed.).

Halas, John. *Masters of Animation.* London: BBC Books, 1987.

Halas, John. *Visual Scripting.* London and New York: Focal Press, 1976.

Harbord, Janet. *La Jetée.* London: Afterall Books, 2009.

Haverty Rugg, Linda. *Picturing Ourselves: Photography and Autobiography.* Chicago, IL: University of Chicago Press, 1997.

Hayward, Stan. *Writing for Animation*. New York: Focal Press, 1977.

Heath, Stephen. "On Screen, in Frame: Film and Ideology" in *Quarterly Review of Film Studies* 1:3. London: Routledge, 1976.

Hemingway, Ernest. *Death in the Afternoon*. London: Arrow Books, 2004.

Hemingway, Ernest. *The Dangerous Summer*. London: Guild Publishing: 1985.

Hess, Thomas B. and John Ashbery. *Narrative Art (Art News Annual XXVI)*. New York: Macmillan, 1970.

Hockney, David and Martin Gayford. *A History of Pictures*. London: Thames & Hudson, 2016.

Hockney, David. *Secret Knowledge*. London: Thames & Hudson, 2006.

Holbein, Hans the Younger. *The Dance of Death*. New York: Dover, 1971.

Honess Roe, Annabelle. *Animated Documentary*. London, New York: Palgrave Macmillan, 2013.

Hongisto, Ilona. *Soul of the Documentary*. Amsterdam: Amsterdam University Press, 2015.

Horton, Andrew S. *Comedy/Cinema/Theory*. Berkeley and Los Angeles: University of California Press, 1991.

Huffman, Eddie—quoted in: https://www.telegraph.co.uk/culture/music/worldfolkandjazz/11464892/John-Prine-biography-review.html retrieved 10–11–19.

Huizinga, Johan. *Homo Ludens: A Study of the Play-Element in Culture*. Kettering, OH: Angelico Press, 2016.

Hutchinson, Garrie (ed.) *The Awful Australian*. South Yarra: Curry O'Neil Ross, 1984.

Jenkins, Eric S. "Another *Punctum*: Animation, Affect and Ideology." *Critical Inquiry*, 39.3 Spring 2013. 575–591.

Jones, Chuck. *Duck Amuck: The Life and Times of an Animated Cartoonist*. New York: Avon Books, 1989.

Jung, C.G. (ed.) *Man and His Symbols*. New York: Dell, 1968.

Jung, C.G. (ed.) *Memories, Dreams, Reflections*. London: Collins, 2020.

Khoo, Olivia, Belinda Small, Audrey Yu. *Transnational Australian Cinema: Ethics in the Asian Diasporas*. Lanham, MD: Lexington Books, 2013.

King, Jonathan. *Stop Laughing, This Is Serious!* Stanmore, NSW: Cassell Australia, 1978.

Klein, Norman. *Seven Minutes: The Life and Death of the American Animated Cartoon*. London, New York: Verso, 1993.

Kornyei, Oscar. "Australia's Greatest Bucking Bull Dies". *The Courier Mail*. Brisbane: 9-1-1997. 3.

Kracauer, Siegfried. *The Mass Ornament: Weimar Essays*. Cambridge, MA: Harvard University Press, 1995.

Kriger, Judith. *Animated Realism: A Behind-the-Scenes Look at the Animated Documentary Genre*. Waltham, MA: Focal Press, 2012.

Kubin, Alfred. *Kubin's Dance of Death and Other Drawings*. New York: Dover, 1973.

Kübler-Ross, Elisabeth. *On Death and Dying*. London: Tavistock, 1970.

Laybourne, Kit. *The Animation Book*. New York: Crown Publishers, 1979.

Leslie, Esther. *Hollywood Flatlands: Animation, Critical Theory and the Avant-garde*. London: Verso, 2002.

Leunig, Mary. *There's No Place Like Home*. Ringwood: Penguin, 1982.

Leunig, Michael. *The Essential Leunig*. Melbourne: Penguin/Viking, 2012.

Leyda, Jay (ed.) *Eisenstein on Disney*. London: Methuen, 1988.

Lifton, Robert Jay. *The Broken Connection: On Death and the Continuity of Life*. New York, Basic Books, 1983.

Lindsay, Joan. *Picnic at Hanging Rock*. Melbourne: FW Cheshire, 1967.

Lipton, Lenny. *Independent Filmmaking*. San Francisco: Straight Arrow Books, 1972.

Lowry, Malcolm. *Under the Volcano*. London: Jonathan Cape, 1947.

Lucie-Smith, Edward. *The Waking Dream: Fantasy and the Surreal in Graphic Art 1450–1900*. New York: Knopf, 1975.

Lupton, Catherine. *Chris Marker: Memories of the Future*. London: Reaktion Books, 2005.

Lutz, E.G. *Animated Cartoons: How They Are Made, Their Origin and Development*. New York: Charles Scribner's Sons, 1920.

Lynch, Jay. *The Best of Bijou Funnies*. London: Omnibus, 1975.

Macdonald, Kevin and Mark Cousins. *Imagining Reality*. London, Boston: Faber and Faber, 1996.

Madsen, Roy P. *Animation: Concepts, Methods, Uses*. New York: Interland, 1969.

Mander, Jerry. *Four Arguments for the Elimination of Television*. New York: William Morrow, 1978.

Mast, Gerald, Marshall Cohen and Leo Braudy (eds). *Film Theory and Criticism*. New York, Oxford: Oxford University Press, 1992.

Mast, Gerald. *The Comic Mind: Comedy and the Movies*. Chicago, IL: University of Chicago Press, 1979.

McClain, David. "Camera Lucida: Select Terms Defined." http://www.davidmcclain.com/TERMS.pdf accessed 20-5-2020.

McCormick, John and Mario Sevilla Mascarenas. *The Complete Aficionado*. Cleveland, OH: World Publishing, 1967.

Medwin, Thomas. *The Life of Percy Bysshe Shelley*. Vol. 1. London: Thomas Cautley Newby, 1847.

Meltzer, David (ed.) *Death: An Anthology of Ancient Texts, Songs, Prayers, and Stories*. San Francisco, CA: North Point Press, 1985.

Monro, D.H. *Argument of Laughter*. Carlton: Melbourne University Press, 1951.

Moses, Gavriel. *The Nickel Was for the Movies: Film in the Novel from Pirandello to Puig*. Berkeley: University of California Press, 1995.

Müller, Peter and Daniele Carbonel. *Costumes of Light*. New York: Assouline, 2004.

Mulvey, Laura. *Death 24x a Second*. London: Reaktion Books, 2006.

Murray, Jonathan and Nea Ehrlich. *Drawn From Life: Issues and Themes in Animated Documentary Cinema*. Edinburgh: Edinburgh University Press, 2020.

Murray, Nicholas. *World Enough and Time: The Life of Andrew Marvell*. London: Little, Brown, 1999.

Muybridge, Eadweard. *Animals in Motion*. New York: Dover, 1957.

Muybridge, Eadweard. *The Human Figure in Motion*. New York: Dover, 1955.

Mynott, Vicki. *Darra By Decade 1820–2010*. Brisbane: Richlands, Inala & Suburbs History Group Inc., 2010.

Nichols, Bill. *Introduction to Documentary*. Bloomington: Indiana University Press, 2010.

Nichols, Bill. *Representing Reality: Issues and Concepts in Documentary*. Bloomington: Indiana University Press, 1991.

Noake, Roger. *Animation: A Guide to Animated Film Techniques*. London: Macdonald Orbis, 1988.

Nuland, Sherwin B. *How We Die*. London: Chatto& Windus, 1994.

Oxford Dictionary of Quotations. Oxford University Press, 1999.

Pelzer, Olga Wiktoria. *Die Filme Dennis Tupicoffs: Zwischen Dokumentar—und Animationsfilm*. Thesis submitted for Magistra der Philosophie (Mag. phil.) at University of Vienna, 2015.

Perisic, Zoran. *The Animation Stand: Rostrum Camera Operations*. London and New York: Focal Press, 1976.

Petty, Bruce. *Petty's Australia—And How It Works*. Ringwood: Penguin, 1976.

Pikkov, Ulo. *Animasophy: Theoretical Writings on the Animated Film*. Tallinn: Estonian Academy of Arts, 2010.

Pilling, Jayne. *A Reader in Animation Studies*. Sydney: John Libbey, 1997.

Pilling, Jayne. *Animation: 2D and Beyond*. Crans-Pres-Celigny, Switzerland: RotoVision SA, 2001.

Pinder, Phil (writer/editor). *Down Underground Comix*. Ringwood: Penguin, 1983.

Pirandello, Luigi. *Shoot! (The Notebooks of Serafino Gubbio)*. Sawtry: Dedalus, 1990.

Pollard, Arthur. *Satire*. London: Methuen, 1970.

Postman, Neil. *Amusing Ourselves to Death*. London: Methuen, 1987.

Powell, Michael. *A Life in Movies*. London: Heinemann, 1986.

Prine, John. *Sweet Revenge*. Atlantic Records, 1973.

Prine, John. *The Tree of Forgiveness*. Oh Boy Records, 2018.

Rehder, William and Gordon Dillow. *Where the Money Is*. New York: W.W. Norton, 2003.

Renov, Michael (ed.) *Theorizing Documentary*. New York, London: Routledge, 1993.

Robinson, Chris. *Ballad of a Thin Man: In Search of Ryan Larkin*. Los Angeles, CA: AWN Press, 2009.

Robinson, Chris. *Unsung Heroes of Animation.* Eastley, UK: John Libbey, 2005.

Rothenstein, Julian (ed). *J.G Posada: Messenger of Mortality.* London: Redstone Press, 1989.

Rowlandson, Thomas and "Doctor Syntax". *The English Dance of Death* Vols. 1&2. London: Methuen, 1903.

Russell, Catherine. *Narrative Mortality.* Minneapolis: University of Minnesota Press, 1995.

Russett, Robert and Cecile Starr. *Experimental Animation: An Illustrated Anthology.* New York: Van Nostrand Reinhold, 1976.

Sacks, Oliver. Review of *A Matter of Life and Death* (Diane Broadbent Friedman) in *The Lancet.* Vol. 373, Issue 9668, March 21 2009 https://www.thelancet.com/journals/lancet/article/PIIS0140-6736(09)60593-6/fulltext accessed 28-6-20.

Salt, Brian G.D. *Movements in Animation (Vol. I).* Oxford: Pergamon. 1976.

Salt, Brian G.D. *Programmes for Animation.* Oxford: Pergamon. 1976.

Schermer, Gerben and Eric van Drunen. "The Animated Documentary: Fiction or Reality?" in *International Documentary Film Festival Amsterdam Catalogue.* Amsterdam: IDFA, 2007: 178–186.

Schiff, Gert. *Images of Horror and Fantasy.* London: Academy Editions, 1980.

Sobchack, Vivian. *Carnal Thoughts: Embodiment and Moving Image Culture.* Berkeley: University of California Press, 2004.

Solnit, Rebecca. *Motion Studies: Time, Space and Eadweard Muybridge.* London: Bloomsbury, 2003.

Solomon, Charles (ed). *The Art of the Animated Image: An Anthology.* Los Angeles, CA: The American Film Institute, 1987.

Solomon, Charles and Ron Stark. *The Complete Kodak Animation Book.* Rochester, NY: Eastman Kodak, 1983.

Solomon, Stanley. *The Film Idea.* New York: Harcourt Brace Jovanovich, 1972.

Spiegl, Fritz (ed). *A Small Book of Grave Humour.* London, Sydney: Pan Books, 1971.

Steadman, Ralph. *Between the Eyes.* London: Jonathan Cape, 1984.

Stephenson, Ralph. *The Animated Film.* London: The Tantivy Press, 1973.

Stevens, Peter S. *Patterns in Nature.* Harmondsworth: Penguin, 1976.

Sulak, Marcela and Jacqueline Kolosov. *Family Resemblance: An Anthology and Exploration of 8 Hybrid Literary Genres.* Brookline, MA: Rose Metal Press, 2015.

Sullivan, Garrett A. Jr. "'More Than Cool Reason Ever Comprehends': Shakespeare, Imagination and Distributed Auteurism in *A Matter of Life and Death."* *Shakespeare Bulletin,* 34.3 Fall 2016. 373–389.

Sutton William and Edward Linn. *Where the Money Was: The Memoirs of a Bank Robber.* New York: Library of Larceny/Broadway Books, 2004.

Sutton, Damian. *Photography Cinema Memory: The Crystal Image of Time*. Minneapolis: University of Minnesota Press, 2009.

Swift, Jonathan. *A Modest Proposal*. https://www.gutenberg.org/files/1080/1080-h/ 1080-h.htm accessed 5-2-20.

Szymborska, Wislawa. *View with a Grain of Sand: Selected Poems*. Orlando: Harvest, 1995.

Taylor, Richard. *The Encyclopedia of Animation Techniques*. East Roseville, NSW: Simon and Schuster, 1996.

Thomas, Frank and Ollie Johnston. *Disney Animation: The Illusion of Life*. New York: Abbeville Press, 1981.

Topor, Roland. *Dessins*. Paris: Albin Michel. 1968.

Topor, Roland. *Le Grand Macabre*. Paris: Hubschmid & Bouret, 1981.

Torre, Dan and Lienors Torre. *Australian Animation: An International History*. Cham, Switzerland: Palgrave Macmillan, 2018.

Torre, Dan. *Animation—Process, Cognition and Actuality*. New York: Bloomsbury Academic, 2017.

Tupicoff, Dennis. "How to Write a Screenplay with a Chainsaw". *Journal of Screenwriting*, 9: 3 (2018): 279–295.

Tupicoff, Dennis. "Radio With Pictures (Thousands of Them): His Mother's Voice". *Cartoons: The International Journal of Animation, 1:1* (Summer 2005): 11–13.

Ungerer, Tomi. *The Underground Sketchbook of Tomi Ungerer*. New York: Dover, 1964.

Ungerer, Tomi. *Tomi Ungerer*. Köln: Argos Press, 1981.

Wahlberg, Malin. *Documentary Time: Film and Phenomenology*. Minneapolis: University of Minnesota Press, 2008.

Ward, Paul. *Documentary: The Margins of Reality*. London: Wallflower, 2005.

Weir, Peter (dir.) *Picnic at Hanging Rock*. (1975) McElroy & McElroy Productions.

Wells, Paul and Johnny Hardstaff. *Re-imaging Animation: The Changing Face of the Moving Image*. Lausanne: Ava, 2008.

Wells, Paul. *Animation: Genre and Authorship*. London: Wallflower, 2002.

Wells, Paul. *Basics of Animation: Scriptwriting*. Lausanne: Ava, 2007.

Wells, Paul. *Understanding Animation*. London, New York: Routledge, 1998.

Whitaker, Harold and John Halas. *Timing for Animation*. London, New York: Focal Press, 1981.

White, Patrick. *The Tree of Man*. London: Penguin, 1963.

White, Tony. *The Animator's Workbook*. New York: Watson Guptill, 1988.

Williams, Richard. *The Animator's Survival Kit*. London and New York: Faber and Faber, 2001.

Wolff, Tobias. *Our Story Begins*. London: Bloomsbury, 2009.

Wright, Thomas. *A History of Caricature and Grotesque in Literature and Art [1865]*. New York: Ungar, 1968.

Zemeckis, Robert., interviewed by Anwar Brett http://www.bbc.co.uk/films/2004/12/01/robert_zemeckis_the_polar_express_interview.shtml retrieved 14–5–20.

Zinn, Christopher. "Obituary: Kerry Packer." https://www.theguardian.com/news/2005/dec/28/guardianobituaries.cricket retrieved 4-3-2020.

Zolnierkiewicz, Teresa. "An Animated Death: Dennis Tupicoff". *Follow Me* (Aug/Sept 1986): 80.

****

FILMS CITED

Features & TV Series

Antonioni, Michelangelo. *Blowup*. (1966) Premier Productions, MGM. 111 minutes.

Batchelor, Joy and John Halas. *Animal Farm*. (1954) Halas & Batchelor. 72 minutes.

Bergman, Ingmar. *The Seventh Seal* (1957) prod: Allan Ekelund. 96 minutes.

Bird, Brad. *Ratatouille*. (2007) Disney/Pixar. 111 minutes.

Burton, Tim, Mike Johnson (dirs). *Corpse Bride* (2005) Prod: Warner Bros. 77 minutes.

Cochrane, Fiona (dir). *All In Her Stride*. (2014) F-reel Productions. 55 minutes.

Daves, Delbert. *Dark Passage* (1947) Warner Bros. 106 minutes.

Donen, Stanley and Gene Kelly. *Singin' in the Rain*. ((1952) MGM. 103 minutes.

Folman, Ari. *Waltz with Bashir*. (2008) Bridgit Folman Film Gang. 90 minutes.

Geronimi, Clyde et al. *101 Dalmatians*. (1961) Walt Disney Productions. 79 minutes.

Gilliam, Terry (animation director) *And Now for Something Completely Different*. Playboy Productions, Kettledrum Films, Lownes Productions. 88 minutes.

Gilliam, Terry (animation director) *Monty Python's Flying Circus*. BBC, Python (Monty) Pictures. (TV Series 1969–1974) 46 episodes × 30 minutes.

Gist, Robert. *An American Dream*. (1966) William Conrad Productions. 103 minutes.

Haas, Clark. *Clutch Cargo*. (1959) Cambria Productions. 52 × 4 minutes.

Hand, David et al. *Bambi*. (1942) Walt Disney Productions. 70 minutes.

Hand, David et al. *Snow White and the Seven Dwarfs*. (1937) Walt Disney Productions. 83 minutes.

Hitchcock, Alfred. *Blackmail*. (1929) BIP 85 minutes.

Hitchcock, Alfred. *Rear Window*. (1954) Patron Inc. 112 minutes.

Hitchcock, Alfred. *Strangers on a Train*. *(1951)* Transatlantic Pictures. 101 minutes.

Hitchcock, Alfred. *Vertigo*. (1958) Alfred J.Hitchcock Productions. 128 minutes.

Huston, John. *Under the Volcano* (1984) Conacite Uno. 112 minutes.

Keaton, Buster and Clyde Bruckman. *The General.* (1926) Keaton/Schenck Productions. 75 minutes.

Konchalovsky, Andrei. *Runaway Train.* (1985) Northbrook/Golan-Globus Productions. 110 minutes.

Laughton, Charles. *The Night of the Hunter* (1955) United Artists. 92 minutes.

Linklater, Richard. *A Scanner Darkly.* (2006) Warner Independent. 100 minutes.

Linklater, Richard. *Waking Life.* (2001) Thousand Words. 101 minutes.

Marker, Chris. *Sans Soleil / Sunless.* (1983) Argos Film. 100 minutes.

Maté, Rudolph. *D.O.A.* (1950) Harry Popkin Productions. 83 minutes.

Montgomery, Robert. *The Lady in the Lake.* (1946) MGM. 112 minutes.

Murnau, F.W. *The Last Laugh* (1924) UFA. 90 minutes.

Peckinpah, Sam. *The Wild Bunch.* (1969) Warner Bros./Seven Arts. 135 minutes.

Penn, Arthur. *Bonnie and Clyde* (1967) Warner Bros./Seven Arts. 111 minutes.

Powell, Michael and Emeric Pressburger (writers/directors/producers). *A Matter of Life and Death.* (1946) The Archers. 104 minutes.

Renoir, Jean. *La Règle du Jeu/The Rules of the Game.* (1939) Nouvelle Édition Française. 110 minutes.

Rosen, Martin. *Watership Down.* (1978) Nepenthe, Watership. 91 minutes.

Selick, Henry. *Tim Burton's The Nightmare Before Christmas.* (1993) Touchstone, Skellington, Tim Burton. 76 minutes.

Sturges, Preston (wr/dir) *Sullivan's Travels.* (1941) Paramount. 90 minutes.

Unkrich, Lee, Adrian Molina. *Coco* (2017) Pixar/Disney. 105 minutes.

Weir, Peter (dir). Picnic at Hanging Rock. (1975) McElroy & McElroy Productions.

Welles, Orson. *Citizen Kane.* (1941) RKO. 119 minutes.

Wiseman, Frederick. *National Gallery.* (2014) 180 minutes.

Wiseman, Frederick. *Titicut Follies* (1967) 84 minutes.

Zemeckis, Robert. *The Polar Express.* (2004) Castle Rock. 100 minutes.

Zemeckis, Robert. *Who Framed Roger Rabbit?* (1988) Touchstone/Amblin/Silver Screen. 104 minutes.

Shorts

Avery, Tex. *A Wild Hare* (1940) Warner Bros. 8 minutes.

Avery, Tex. *Lonesome Lenny.* (1946) MGM. 8 minutes.

Barrett, Shirley. *Chainsaw: Bull Born Bad* (1991) Film Australia. 30 minutes.

Cohl, Émile. *Fantasmagorie.* (1908) 2 minutes.

Cournoyer, Michele. *The Hat.* (1999) NFB Canada. 6 minutes.

Enrico, Robert. *An Occurrence at Owl Creek Bridge* (1961) Filmartic, Les Films du Centaure. 28 minutes.

Fleischer, Dave. *Minnie the Moocher* (1933) Fleischer Studios. 8 minutes.

Fleischer, Max and Dave Fleischer. *Out of the Inkwell* (1918–1929) Fleischer Studios.

Franju, Georges. *Le Sang des bêtes /Blood of the Beasts*. (1949) Forces et voix de la France. 22 minutes.

Freleng, Friz. *Greedy for Tweety* (1957) Warner Bros. 6 minutes.

Gillett, Burt. *Playful Pluto*.(1934) Walt Disney. 8 minutes.

Hertzfeldt, Don (dir). *Rejected* (2000) Bitter Films. 10 minutes.

Hodgson, Jonathan. *Feeling My Way* (1997) 6 minutes.

Hodgson, Jonathan. *Night Club* (1983) 6 minutes.

Hubley, John and Faith. *Moonbird*. (1959) 10 minutes.

Iwerks, Ub. *Skeleton Dance*. (1929) Walt Disney. 6 minutes.

Jones, Chuck. *Bully for Bugs*. (1953) Warner Bros. 7 minutes.

Jones, Chuck. *Don't Give Up the Sheep* (1953) etc: *Wolf and Sheep Dog* series. (1953–1963) Warner Bros. 7 minutes.

Jones, Chuck. *Fast and Furry-ous* (1949) etc: *Wile E. Coyote and Roadrunner* series (1949–1965) Warner Bros. 7 minutes.

Landreth, Chris. *Ryan*. (2004) Copperheart, NFB Canada. 14 minutes.

Lavis, Chris & Maciek Szczerbowski. *Madame Tutli-Putli* (2007) NFB Canada. 17 minutes.

Lingford, Ruth. *Death and the Mother* (2000) Channel 4. 10 minutes.

Lumiere, August and Louis. *L'arrivée d'un train en gare de La Ciotat*. (1896) 1 minute.

Marker, Chris. *La Jetée* (1962) Argos Films, RTF. 28 minutes.

McCay, Winsor. *Gertie the Dinosaur*. (1914) Universal. 12 minutes.

McCay, Winsor. *Little Nemo*. (1911) Vitagraph, 11 minutes.

McCay, Winsor. *The Sinking of the Lusitania*. (1918) Universal. 12 minutes.

McKimson, Robert. *Devil May Hare*. (1954) Warner Bros. 7 minutes.

McLaren, Norman. *Neighbours*. (1952) NFB Canada. 8 minutes.

Moyes, Peter. *Sunday* (1992) Dumbshow. 3 minutes.

Petty, Bruce. *Australian History*. (1971) 10 minutes.

Petty, Bruce. *Leisure*. (1976) Film Australia. 14 minutes.

Sabiston, Bob. *Grasshopper*. (2004) Flat Black Films. 14 minutes.

Sabiston, Bob. *Snack and Drink*. (1999) Flat Black Films. 4 minutes.

Index

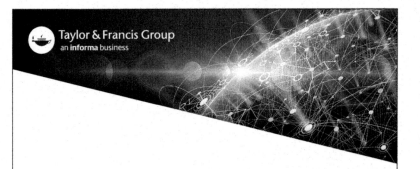